FAITHFULNESS

by:

Dr. Ricky Edwards

© 2019 Ricky Edwards All Rights Reserved. Unauthorized Duplication is Prohibited.

Copyright © 2019 Ricky Edwards. United States of America. All Rights Reserved under international copyright laws. Contents and/or cover may not be reproduced in whole or in part without prior written consent.

Printed in the United States of America

Published by Aion Multimedia
20118 N 67th Ave
Suite 300-446
Glendale AZ 85308
www.aionmultimedia.com

ISBN-13: 978-1-7330332-2-0

Scripture quotations taken from the Amplified® Bible (AMP), Copyright © 2015 by The Lockman Foundation. Used by permission. (www.Lockman.org)

Scripture quotations taken from the Amplified® Bible, Classic Edition are marked (AMPC), Copyright © 1954, 1958, 1962, 1964, 1965, 1987 by The Lockman Foundation. Used by permission." (www.Lockman.org)

Unless otherwise indicated, all Scripture quotations marked (BBE) are taken from the public domain version of The Bible in Basic English as presented on http://www.biblestudytools.com/bbe/.

Scripture quotations taken from the Common English Bible are marked (CEB), as presented at https://www.biblegateway.com/versions/Common-English-Bible-CEB/#booklist Copyright 2012 by Common English Bible and are used in accordance with the 1976 Copyright Act, the 1998 Digital Millennium Copyright Act

Scripture quotations taken from the Contemporary English Version® are marked (CEV), Copyright © 1995 American Bible Society. All rights reserved.

Scripture is taken from GOD'S WORD® are marked (GW), © 1995 God's Word to the Nations. Used by permission of Baker Publishing Group.

Unless otherwise indicated, all Scripture quotations marked (KJV) are taken from the public domain King James Version of the Bible as presented on https://www.biblegateway.com/versions/King-James-Version-KJV-Bible/ .

Scripture taken from The Message are marked (MSG). Copyright © 1993, 1994, 1995, 1996, 2000, 2001, 2002. Used by permission of NavPress Publishing Group.

Scripture quotations taken from the New American Standard Bible® (NASB), Copyright © 1960, 1962, 1963, 1968, 1971, 1972, 1973, 1975, 1977, 1995 by The Lockman Foundation Used by permission. www.Lockman.org

Unless otherwise indicated, all Scripture taken from the New King James Version® is marked (NKJV). Copyright © 1982 by Thomas Nelson. Used by permission. All rights reserved.

Scripture quotations marked (NLT) are taken from the Holy Bible, New Living Translation, copyright © 1996, 2004, 2007 by Tyndale House Foundation. Used by permission of Tyndale House Publishers, Inc., Carol Stream, Illinois 60188. All rights reserved.

Scripture quotations marked (TLB) are taken from The Living Bible copyright © 1971 by Tyndale House Foundation. Used by permission of Tyndale House Publishers Inc., Carol Stream, Illinois 60188. All rights reserved. The Living Bible, TLB, and the The Living Bible logo are registered trademarks of Tyndale House Publishers

Unless otherwise indicated, all Scripture quotations marked (WNT) are taken from the public domain Weymouth New Testament in Modern Speech, Third Edition 1913, as presented on http://www.biblestudytools.com/wnt/.

TABLE OF CONTENTS

Preface	i
Study Tips	i
Helpful Formatting Notes	iii
Introduction	v
PART ONE - FAITHFULNESS	1
CHAPTER 1 - THE IMPORTANCE OF BEING LED	3
Outward Signs	3
The Inward Witness	4
Don't Get Fleeced	6
New Testament Prophecy Works with the Inward Witness	9
Guided Tour vs. Self-Guided Tour	10
CHAPTER 2 - GOD'S IDEA OF FAITHFULNESS	13
Biblical Faithfulness	13
The Potter and the Clay	14
Understanding God's Order	16
The Natural Is the Training Ground for the Supernatural	17
Faithfulness Is the Key to Promotion	18
CHAPTER 3 - EXAMPLES OF FAITHFULNESS	21
The Unfaithful King	21
The Faithful Boy	25
Our Own Faithfulness Journey	31
CHAPTER 4 - FAITHFULNESS REQUIRES TRUST	37
Abraham Trusted God	37
Noah Trusted God	40
We Trusted God	41
CHAPTER 5 - FAITHFULNESS REQUIRES TRAINING	43
Do Not Despise Small Beginnings	43
The More You Walk, the Better You'll Walk	44
Training Faithfully	45
CHAPTER 6 - FAITHFULNESS REQUIRES OBEDIENCE	49
Can You Follow Directions?	49
The Ark of the Covenant	51

Faithfulness to God and Men	53
There's a Place for Every Believer	57
CHAPTER 7 - FAITHFULNESS WITH MONEY	**61**
Obey in the Small Things and Receive the Big Things	61
Money Is a Small Thing	63
The Importance of the Tithe	65
CHAPTER 8 - FAITHFULNESS REQUIRES TESTING	**69**
Training Requires Testing	69
The Test of Things	71
"These Ten Times"	72
CHAPTER 9 - THE HEART OF FAITHFULNESS	**77**
Faithfulness in the Hard Places	77
The Heart Issue	78
Natural Talent Does Not Supersede Faithfulness	81
Is Your Fur Rubbed Wrong?	82
CHAPTER 10 - A DEEPER LOOK AT FAITHFULNESS	**85**
Living the Good Life	85
Settle it in Your Heart to Complete the Process	87
Don't Rush but Don't Delay	89
Be Patient and Alert	91
Be Ready to Course Correct	93
CHAPTER 11 - FAITHFULNESS AND THE BLESSING	**95**
The BLESSING of God	95
The BLESSING Is More Than Just Money	98
The BLESSING Makes You Rich	100
CHAPTER 12 - INCREASE FOLLOWS FAITHFULNESS	**103**
Benefits Follow Faithfulness	103
Faithfulness to God Brings Increase	105
The Anointing Is Tied to Faithfulness	106
PART TWO- OPEN DOORS AND MINISTRY ROOMS	**111**
CHAPTER 13 - THE OPEN DOOR BEFORE YOU	**113**
The Increase on the Other Side	113
Faithfulness Is the Key	115
Don't Compare Doors	118
CHAPTER 14 - DIFFICULTIES AT THE DOOR	**119**
The Adversaries at the Open Door	120

Familiar Spirits—Satan's Reconnaissance Team	121
Doors for Personal Growth Can Be Uncomfortable	123
Corporate Doorways and Corporate Adversaries	124
CHAPTER 15 - MINISTRY ROOMS AND PHASES	**127**
Ministry Gifts and the Importance of a Shepherd	127
Ministry Phases and Rooms	129
All Ministries Have Phases and Rooms	132
CHAPTER 16 - MORE ABOUT THE ANOINTING	**139**
A Taste of Your Future	139
The Personal Anointing vs. Anointing for Ministry	141
Don't Shipwreck Your Faith	143
CHAPTER 17 - FINAL THOUGHTS	**147**
We Must Faithfully Continue Until Jesus Returns	148
Confession of Faithfulness	150
APPENDIX 1 - THE PLAN OF SPIRITUAL SALVATION	**151**
BIBLIOGRAPHY	**155**

Matthew 25:21 (NKJV)

²¹ His lord said to him, "Well done, good and faithful servant; you were faithful over a few things, I will make you ruler over many things. Enter into the joy of your lord."

(All emphasis in Scriptures have been added by the author.)

PREFACE

STUDY TIPS

None of us know everything there is to know about the things of God. Sometimes a preacher or teacher's revelation and knowledge are so deep on a subject it will throw someone off. Brother Kenneth Hagin, the founder of Rhema Bible Training Center ("Rhema"), was notorious for that. He never intentionally tried to confuse people. But the depth of the revelation he walked in would cause people to say, "Really? Where did that come from?" None of us know everything, but the Holy Ghost in us does. We can be thankful for that. As we listen to Him and follow Him, we'll be able to grow and mature.

Along those lines, any time a preacher begins teaching on issues dealing with the soulish realm or the flesh, people get a little wiggly because it is uncomfortable. Likewise, if a preacher brings something people haven't heard before, or that goes against a sacred doctrine they've been taught, they want to reject it outright. Sometimes the Holy Ghost will show a person something through a teacher or a preacher that is a little bit ahead of where they are right now because He understands something is coming, and they'll need this information when the situation arrives. When these things happen to you, always try to understand that the Holy Ghost is doing His best through a human vessel to get answers to you. That way, when you get there, you will be prepared and the outcome will be different.

Jesus told us, "Heaven and earth will pass away, but the Word of God is forever[1]." The Bible is our safety net because we know that the WORD of God never changes[2]. Any time a lesson is taught, a message is preached, or a word is given, it must agree with the WORD of God—never solely

---

[1] Matthew 24:35
[2] Isaiah 55:11; Numbers 23:19; Malachi 3:6; Hebrews 13:8

based on someone's experience or opinion. Everything taught must agree with Scripture.

For example, I've had angels show up in my meetings. But if an angel or a supernatural being walked through a wall and stood right before me all glowing and said, "There is no longer going to be a rapture of the Church," even though he's supernatural, I wouldn't accept that because it goes against the WORD of God which says there will be a catching away in the air[3]. We know Jesus is coming back for us. So if I have a visitation from an angelic being and they tell me something, it better line up with the WORD. Because if it doesn't, then they aren't sent by God. Even though he is supernatural, his message is not consistent with the WORD. Everything has to come back to the WORD—every time.

So, before you read, I ask you to pray and ask God to open the eyes of your understanding. If you are born again and filled with the Holy Ghost as evidenced by speaking in other tongues, then pray in the Spirit for a few minutes before you read. Some of this material may seem difficult to understand at first. But, with the help of the Holy Spirit, I'll do my best to keep it simple. Don't settle for confusion and don't give up.

As you are reading, be sure you have your own Bibles next to you and look up every single Scripture. I'll have them in the King James Version (KJV), or another version that I frequently use in my meetings, but it's important for you to fact check everything. This is especially important if you generally use a different translation. Additionally, read each Scripture aloud. According to Romans 10:17, *"Faith comes by hearing."* When you read God's WORD aloud, it gets deeper into your heart because you are engaging your whole self—spirit, soul, and body. Your mind cannot wander when it must concentrate on what it sees, hears, and speaks all at one time. That's when your spirit man is in control rather than your soul or your flesh.

---

[3] 1 Thessalonians 4:14-17

As you progress through the material, read a section and meditate on it before moving on. Make sure you truly understand what the Spirit of God is saying. As Isaiah 1:19 promises, *"If ye be willing and obedient, ye shall eat the good of the land"* (KJV). That means, if you will dig into this material and not settle for any confusion, you will experience a deeper revelation and understanding that will bring you greater victory.

HELPFUL FORMATTING NOTES

It is often helpful to understand the thought processes behind the layout of a book of this nature. We have divided each chapter into smaller more manageable sections. Don't worry about reading a whole chapter in one sitting. Allow yourself to enjoy one section at a time and truly digest this material.

Because we believe all Scripture is the inerrant WORD of God and Jesus is the very LOGOS (3056.Logos) or divine utterance of God[4], we capitalize WORD when referring to the WORD of God. Along the same lines, LORD is also completely capitalized to honor Jesus as the one who paid the ransom for our spirits with His very blood (2962.Kurios). Additionally, all pronouns referring to God, Holy Spirit, and Jesus are capitalized as well.

Scriptures are handled four ways in this book:

1. The main Scripture references discussed are inset from both margins and displayed in *italics* with important phrases in ***bold***.

2. Other Scriptures, if quoted exactly, are shown in quotations and italics, and are usually found within the paragraph itself.

3. If Scriptures are presented in the "Ricky paraphrase" they are given in quotations, but not in italics. The reference will be given in the footnotes.

---
[4] John 1:1-16

4. When the scriptural proof is presented for a doctrinal statement, the appropriate Scripture references are usually listed in a footnote on the same page.

It is important to note that we have endeavored to list a reference for every Scripture whether directly quoted or paraphrased because our goal is to be as scripturally accurate as possible. We have also endeavored to provide a complete bibliography should you wish to dig deeper into any of these subjects.

INTRODUCTION

I appreciate each of you taking the time to pick up this book. Each of us has plenty of things to be doing. But you are choosing to go after something God has for you. That is not lost on me. I appreciate you taking the time to obey God to read it. God had a reason for me to write it, and He has a reason for you to read it. [5]

In case this is your first experience with me, let me share a little about myself. I grew up in the church. My mom and dad were very good Christian people. They raised us in the Assemblies of God, and they always lived out at home what they did at the church building. When I was a kid, Mother became ill. At that time, we all prayed according to the light of the WORD we had which was, "God, if it be Your will, please heal Ruthie." So many people were praying for my mom, but she died.

As a result of my mother's death, many different things happened to me. When I was 16, I left the church and became the town drunk. For eight years of my life, I don't really know where I was or what I did except that I was really good friends with the Po-Po[6]. They drove me around a lot; I was in the backseat and they were in the front. I spent a lot of time in jail and almost went to prison. I wasn't even living at the bottom of the barrel[7]. You could pretty much say I was living underneath it. There's not much I remember from that time. But that's okay. I don't even care to, because that old man is dead. I've been redeemed from all that and made a new creature in Christ Jesus[8]. I'm thankful for what the BLOOD has done, but I'm also thankful for what the WORD will do. Even with

---

[5]

[6] Police

[7] *The bottom of the barrel* is an American idiom meaning that someone is the poorest of the poor, or that something is the very lowest quality. For example, if you consider apples or peaches in a barrel, those at the bottom would be most likely smashed and bruised. Further, by the time you get to those, your supply is very limited (Bottom of the Barrel).

[8] 2 Corinthians 5:17, 21

everything that happened, God still called me, and I'm so grateful for the call.

Dealing with the loss of my mother so young, and growing up in a denominational church, meant I had to overcome and unlearn some things in order to come into the fullness of God's call on my life. The Holy Spirit had to help me with many things over the course of my life and I'm so grateful that He did. The Bible is progressive in revelation. That means as I got revelation in an area, more was revealed. I had to learn to look at some things differently when I came back into fellowship with the LORD. Don't get me wrong. Not everything had to be unlearned; some things were foundational and I just needed to build upon them.

I'm not unique. It works the same for all of us. It doesn't matter if it is additional light received on a subject, or if it is something that was misunderstood, the Bible is still meant to be learned line upon line and precept upon precept[9]. It doesn't all come at once. If it did, most of us wouldn't have enough sense to walk in all of it. It is dangerous to get light and not walk in it. Because once you receive the revelation, you become accountable for it. If you don't walk in it, then it will start working against you rather than for you[10].

I'm sure we can all agree that we live in a time of unprecedented teaching and outpouring of revelation. We have greater light on certain things now than we did just a few years ago. Back then, when we started, we just didn't understand some things. Thank God, the Holy Ghost didn't leave us back there with an incomplete understanding. He wants all of us walking in the fullness of revelation and working with the anointing rather than against it.

The subject of this book—faithfulness—is very close and dear to my heart. It's interesting when you get to digging around in the Scriptures to see what faithfulness truly means. For many Christians, the word *faithfulness* has almost become a cliché. They say, "We're faithful," but they often don't know the true Bible meaning of the word. I was like that. For years, I equated faithfulness with diligence— just showing up—and

---

[9] Isaiah 28:10
[10] More on this later in the book.

Introduction

hard work. Diligence and working hard are good qualities to have. However, in the Scriptures, faithfulness is about so much more than diligence or hard work. My prayer is that this book will help you understand faithfulness the way God understands it. With that in mind, always remember, every improvement we make can only make us better.

Part One – Faithfulness

CHAPTER 1 – THE IMPORTANCE OF BEING LED

What exactly does it mean to be faithful? For years, I was like many other Christians and equated faithfulness with just showing up. Basically, I thought it meant diligence or working hard at something. But God wants us to understand things the way He understands them. Slowly He began to teach me, line upon line and precept upon precept, the true biblical meaning of faithfulness: trusting God enough to do what He asks the way He has it in His heart for it to be done.

> *³⁵ Then I will raise up for Myself a **faithful** priest **who shall do according to what is in My heart and in My mind**. I will build him a sure house, and he shall walk before My anointed forever. (1 Samuel 2:35 NKJV)*

But there is even more to it than just doing what is in God's heart. Being faithful also means being willing to be led. You cannot be faithful to the things of God if you don't know what God has in His heart. That is the job of the Holy Ghost with the inward witness. So before beginning our discussion on faithfulness, I want to spend some time discussing the vitally important concept of being led.

OUTWARD SIGNS

In the denomination I grew up in, we were taught that sometimes God would use sickness, disease, calamity, and other bad stuff to teach people a lesson. I was also taught if you wanted guidance and direction from God to ask for an open or closed door, a sign, or a fleece. Some of you may recognize those teachings as well. Our prayers went, "God, if You want me to do this, then open that door." Or, "God, if You don't want me to do that, then please close that door." We used Revelation 3:8 as our basis for those prayers.

We see an example of this in the book of Judges, Gideon was hiding behind the winepress threshing his wheat when the angel said to him, "Behold, thou mighty man of valor[11]."

Gideon looked around and said, "Who?"

Then the angel told him, "God is going to save Israel by you."

But what did Gideon say? "Me? No, way!"

"No, really, God is going to save them."

"Well, please don't be mad at me, but if it's really You, LORD, then let the fleece be dry and the ground wet in the morning."

The angel gave Gideon what he wanted. But he still wasn't sure he could believe what he was hearing. He asked for the opposite the next morning. Thus, those *fleeces* were outward signs or confirmation that what the angel was telling him was indeed God's plan. In other words, they helped Gideon come to a place where he understood why God made him and what was in God's heart for him to do.

Gideon had to understand God's purpose for his life before he could move out and begin to fulfill that purpose. Of course, eventually, he did believe the angel and went through the open door. He faithfully executed God's plan to deliver Israel from her enemies and from idolatry. He went on to lead Israel faithfully for many years[12].

THE INWARD WITNESS

God allowed the fleece for Gideon because Gideon didn't have the Holy Spirit living inside him to guide him in the steps he should take. But is that how the New Testament Church is to be led? Let's think about this for a moment. We know that in the Old Covenant, there was guidance

---

[11] Judges 6
[12] Judges 6-8

through the office of the prophet[13], and by signs and wonders[14]. There was also guidance through the ephod[15] that the High Priest would wear, and the Urim and Thummim that were carried in it[16]. We also know from Scripture and the story of Gideon, they could put out a fleece[17].

However, it is different for the New Testament Church, because Jesus told the disciples, "You know the Holy Ghost, for He has been *with* you. But there is something different about to happen. Now, He is going to be *inside* you[18]." Why? Because the Holy Ghost couldn't live inside people until after Jesus died and was resurrected.

Say this out loud, "I am a New Testament saint. Since I'm New Testament, I should expect to be led by the Spirit of God living on the *inside* of me."

Why am I telling you all this? Let's take a look at Romans 8:14-16 for the answer:

> *[14] For as many as are **led by the Spirit of God**, they are the sons of God.*
>
> *[15] For ye have not received the spirit of bondage again to fear; but ye have received the Spirit of adoption, whereby we cry, Abba, Father.*
>
> *[16] The Spirit **itself beareth witness with our spirit**, that we are the children of God: (Romans 8:14-16 KJV)*

Look at verse 14 carefully. We are the group verse 14 is talking about. In verse 16, what does the Holy Ghost bear witness with? Our spirit. And, where does He live? On the inside of us. Therefore, those who are led by

---

[13] Exodus 7:1; Deuteronomy 18:18; Matthew 11:13
[14] Exodus 13:21
[15] For an excellent description of the High Priest's ephod, see http://www.templeinstitute.org/beged/priestly_garments-6.htm
[16] Exodus 28:30 (AMPC)
[17] Judges 6:36-40
[18] John 14:17

the Spirit of God are the children of God and the Spirit itself[19] bears witness with our spirit. I am so glad the New Testament reveals the Teacher to the Church—the Holy Ghost! He is a teacher and has been given the responsibility to make sure that you and I are led, taught, guided, and taken care of properly.

We need to study this very carefully. Because if we don't understand it and continue to believe that God teaches with sickness and calamity, or leads with fleeces and open/closed doors, then we are going to get hoodwinked and the devil is going to beat our brains out. Remember, we are the only group that is to be guided by the inward witness—by the Spirit of God inside us. This means outward signs were acceptable under the Old Covenant because no one living at that time could be led by the inward witness. But the Church has a Guide.

DON'T GET FLEECED

So when you pray, "God, *if* You want me to take that new job, *then* let them hire me," you just got fleeced. Because God put your life into His hands. He took on the responsibility to lead you, to guide you, and to teach you. But with that prayer, you just told Him, "I don't want to pay attention to You. I want to be led by everything I can feel, see, and touch."

People come to me all the time and ask, "We know how God uses you. What do you think about this thing we're dealing with? Can you tell us what to do?"

"Well, I probably could, but I won't." This response almost always puzzles them. But I won't because that is a wrong leading.

I wouldn't even tell my own son. He came to me one day because he was in love and wanted to marry this certain girl. We knew her almost her entire life and liked her. So he asked me what I thought. I said, "Do you love her?"

---

[19] Notice *itself*, and keep in mind the Holy Spirit is not an it. He is the third Person of the Trinity.

Chapter 1: The Importance of Being Led

"Yes," he answered quite sincerely.

"Do you want to marry her?"

"Yes. But I have to move to this place. What do you think?" he asked again.

I answered quite frankly, "I don't know. But I think you've got the Holy Ghost on the inside of you."

"Yeah, but I don't want to miss God."

"Well, that would be God who lives on the inside of you as the Holy Ghost."

"Yeah, but can you just tell me what to do?" he persisted.

"I probably could, but I won't."

"Why? Why won't you, Dad?"

"Because I said you have the Holy Ghost on the inside of you. You're not led by your parents. You're not led by fleeces. You're not led by open and closed doors. You're supposed to be led by the Holy Ghost. Start praying."

Now I don't have to pray about things like going to church or walking in love towards others. The Bible is very clear on that. People waste a lot of good oxygen praying about things they don't need to pray about. The Bible is very plain. It tells you to walk in love[20]. It tells you not to forsake the assembly[21]. It also tells you, if you're born again, to be a tither[22]. If you pray to see if you should tithe, you won't hear anything from heaven because God's WORD has already told you to do it.

> *13 Howbeit when he, **the Spirit of truth**, is come, he will guide **you into all truth**: for he shall not speak of himself;*

---

[20] Ephesians 5:1-2
[21] Hebrews 10:25
[22] Mark 12:17

> *but whatsoever he shall hear, **that shall he speak**: and he will shew you things to come. (John 16:13 KJV)*

The *Spirit of truth* is the Holy Ghost. Where is He going to guide you? Into all truth. What will He speak? Only what He hears from God the Father. So if a born-again believer isn't sure about something—say a new job or getting married—and he asks God, "LORD, should I do that? I want to follow You on this." God hears that prayer because the believer went to the Father in Jesus' name.

Father God probably thinks something along the lines of, "I appreciate him asking Me. He wants Me to be involved in everything he does. I am his Dad." God then says to the Holy Ghost, who lives inside the believer, "Go ahead and bear witness with him to do it." The Holy Ghost will do as instructed. The believer won't see anything, hear anything, or feel anything. But inside them, in their spirit, there will be a knowing of what God wants him to do. Then God is obligated, through the Holy Spirit on the inside of the believer, to lead him and guide him in the path he should go to accomplish whatever it is he prayed about[23].

On the flip side, if you ask God to lead you with a sign on the outside, then you could be stepping into a trap. Yes, God is outside of you as well as inside of you. But you have to remember that the devil and his cohorts are outside as well. God does not tolerate sin in His dwelling place or share it with demons[24]. The critical point here is that demons cannot live inside born-again Christians because that is where God lives. If only the inward witness leads you, then there is no way that the devil can get involved in your leading to lead you astray. However, once you pray and ask for an outside leading, the devil can easily arrange for a false sign to trick you.

---

[23] Sometimes,people will get the leading from the Holy Ghost, and they aren't quite sure if it was them or if it was God. Let me assure you, since you have the Holy Ghost inside you, it was you. But it was you by the Spirit of God.

[24] Revelation 12:9 – This topic is addressed more thoroughly in my book *The Soul*.

Say this out loud: "I'm led by the Holy Ghost who lives on the inside of me."

NEW TESTAMENT PROPHECY WORKS WITH THE INWARD WITNESS

You may be wondering about the prophetic gifts that flow in the Church today. One of the things I so appreciated about Dr. Ed Dufresne[25], who became our spiritual father in 2003 after Brother Hagin[26] went to be with the LORD, was that when he gave a word to someone, he would always ask them if it fit, or if they had a witness about it in their spirit. Why did he do that? Because he knew that they had the same Holy Spirit on the inside of them that he did. They didn't operate in the same office, but they had the same Spirit. We are all led by the same Holy Ghost. There isn't one for the fivefold ministry offices and one for the rest of the believers. The same Holy Ghost leads all of us.

We live in a time when we are seeing Bible prophecy being fulfilled before our eyes, seemingly on a daily basis. Not only that, but the revelation being poured out prophetically to the Church seems to be increasing daily as well. Therefore, before we close this discussion on being led, I want to make sure we understand and agree that the New Testament Church is not to be led by prophecy either.

Prophecy can confirm some stuff for us, but we are not led by it. Why not? Well, according to 1 Corinthians 14:3, the simple gift of prophecy that comes through any laity will edify, exhort, and comfort. That's all it is supposed to do. But when you bring prophecy through a higher office, it

---

[25] "Dr. Ed Dufresne was a bold and compassionate minister with over 49 years in the ministry. In 1971, God put a tangible healing anointing in Dr. Dufresne's right hand, and since then he has traveled over 11 million air miles carrying that healing anointing to this generation (Dufresne Ministries)."

[26] Kenneth E. Hagin had a rocky start in life that God used to build great faith. In fact, many call him the father of the modern faith movement. He started preaching at the age of 17 and continued in ministry right up until he went home to be with the LORD. Among his many ministry exploits, Brother Hagin ministered worldwide in All Faith's Crusades and founded Rhema Bible Training College in 1974. (Hagin Memorial)

can bring revelation. Therefore, when the prophecy comes through the office of a prophet or a pastor, it is no longer to just edify, exhort, or comfort. It will carry revelation with it.

Let me illustrate this for you. In Acts 21:9, when Paul was at Philip's house, the Bible records that Philip's four virgin daughters had the gift of prophecy. Yet God sent the prophet, Agabus, to Paul after several days. The girls had the simple gift of prophecy—a helps ministry for their local church— so they never picked up on the message that God had Agabus bring[27].

> *[10] And as we tarried there many days, there came down from Judaea a certain prophet, named Agabus.*
>
> *[11] And when he was come unto us, he took Paul's girdle, and bound his own hands and feet, and said, "Thus saith the Holy Ghost, So shall the Jews at Jerusalem bind the man that owneth this girdle, and shall deliver him into the hands of the Gentiles." (Acts 21:10-11 KJV)*

I think all of us can agree that message did not bring edification, but it did bring revelation. So sometimes, when prophecy comes through the office of the prophet, God will reveal glimpses of your future. But you must still walk it out step by step, being led by the Holy Ghost all along the way.

Always remember, a prophet can confirm some things for you, but you should have the leading of the inward witness first. If something is said and the witness inside you doesn't agree with it, then just put it on the shelf and wait for the leading, or the witness, of the Spirit, because that is always safe.

GUIDED TOUR VS. SELF-GUIDED TOUR

Another trap believers need to watch out for is leading themselves. Years and years ago, when my wife and I lived in Southeast Texas, we

---

[27] Acts 21:8-14

Chapter 1: The Importance of Being Led

took a trip to West Texas and decided to visit Carlsbad Caverns National Park since we were close. When we arrived, they gave us two options for touring the cavern: a guided tour or a self-guided tour. Sally looked at me and immediately said, "No, you're not!"

How many of you reading this book have ever gotten yourself lost? I bet during those times you might have been like me. It wasn't that you didn't know where you were; you just didn't know where you were at that moment, right? Sally wasn't about to take a chance on me getting us lost in a big cave. She wanted someone to guide us through it who knew where we were going.

In this life, there are places to go and things to do. It is the Holy Ghost's job to lead me to the places that I wouldn't necessarily know to go to on my own, or maybe I just wouldn't self-guide myself to. But as I allow Him to lead me, He will always do it with my purpose in mind[28].

My flesh doesn't like to be in a hard place all the time. It likes the easier, softer way. Under the leadership of the Holy Ghost, you might get to singing that old song, "I never promised you a rose garden[29]," because some things might be tough, but that doesn't mean He didn't lead you there.

That's why the book of Ephesians tells us not to grieve the Holy Ghost[30], because many times people will desire to do other things besides follow Him and that grieves Him. It isn't from the point that He's upset because He's not getting His way. Rather, He has been given the responsibility to take care of you and He knows what is down the road on your path.

People try to tell me, "It's hard here." Let me say, as much as I've traveled, I've learned it is hard just about everywhere you go. The truth is,

---
[28] Romans 8:28
[29] "Rose Garden" (also known and covered as "(I Never Promised You a Rose Garden") is a song written by Joe South, best known as recorded by country music singer Lynn Anderson, and first released by Billy Joe Royal in 1967 (Rose Garden).
[30] Ephesians 4:30

if your perspective is right, you'll eventually get to a place where you realize it isn't really hard. It's actually fun—everywhere God sends you. It doesn't matter wherever you go, there will always be a devil. But if God asked you to go there, then you're walking with the power and the anointing, and no weapon formed against you can prosper[31].

A lot of what I'm teaching, I've had to be led through. Romans 8:14 in the Message translation says, *"God's Spirit beckons. There are things to do and places to go!"* That's talking about leading. The Holy Spirit is trying to lead us to and through a door that God has opened for us. We need to follow His leadership of the inward witness. Say this aloud, "I'm being led by the Holy Ghost. There are places to go and things to do and He's the one guiding me."

Maybe some of you have been on a guided hunt before. It is important to understand, if you go somewhere new, just because you have a gun and bullets doesn't mean you're qualified to hunt there. You might be out there for days and never see anything; however, the guide will know where everything is. The Holy Ghost works the same way. He knows things that there is no way you can know naturally, things He knows from God concerning your future. And if God doesn't tell Him to tell you, He will never reveal it to you even though He is still responsible to lead you through it. That's why people get glimpses and inklings of their future—so they won't just camp out somewhere. Rather, these glimpses propel them to follow the leading of the Holy Ghost to get to that next place.

---

[31] Isaiah 54:17

CHAPTER 2 – GOD'S IDEA OF FAITHFULNESS

BIBLICAL FAITHFULNESS

We often call Abraham—born Abram—the father of faith. But what did God call him and why? To understand the true meaning of faithfulness, let's begin by studying this patriarch of faith.

> *⁷ Thou art the LORD the God, **who didst choose Abram**, and broughtest him forth out of Ur of the Chaldees, and gavest him the name of Abraham;*
>
> *⁸ **And foundest his heart faithful before thee**, and madest a covenant with him to give the land of the Canaanites, the Hittites, the Amorites, and the Perizzites, and the Jebusites, and the Girgashites, to give it, I say, to his seed, and hast performed thy words; for thou art righteous. (Nehemiah 9:7-8 KJV)*

This is so precious to me. Who did God choose? Abram (who would later be called Abraham). What did God find in Abram? A faithful heart. Notice the very first thing God had Moses write about was the first test Abram faced. What was it? Leaving Ur and his kinfolk without knowing the final destination[32].

It wasn't like God just looked down one day and said, "Oh! There's Abraham! I found him!" No. He knew where Abraham was all along. It was through asking Abraham to do certain things that God found him to be faithful. In other words, Abraham's consistent obedience showed God he would do everything that God had in His heart. This was a time-consuming process. It didn't happen overnight.

---

[32] Genesis 12:1-3

After enough tests, Abraham got to the place where it didn't matter what God asked him to do. He did it right away. We see this in Genesis 14:11-24 when God gave Abraham the covenant of circumcision. He didn't waste any time. Verse 23 tells us he *"circumcised the flesh of their foreskin in the selfsame day."* He circumcised every single male—not just the ones born in his household, but also the ones who worked for him – the very same day God asked him to do it. This shows faithfulness from a perspective we may not have seen before.

When we closely study Abraham's life, we see God tested him many, many times over the course of 34 years. The first test recorded in Genesis 12:1 was to leave Ur of the Chaldees. Thirty-four years later, the very last test in Genesis 22 was being willing to sacrifice his beloved Isaac. It was over the course of these 34 years that God found Abraham's heart faithful, because that's how long it took Abraham to get to the place where he could trust God with his life and everything he owned, even his beloved son. Now in your Bible, I want you to put a note that says, "This took time," next to that phrase in Nehemiah 9:8: *"And foundest his heart faithful before thee."*

THE POTTER AND THE CLAY

God has a specific plan and purpose for you that is different from every other person who's ever lived. He's not going to ask you to do something just to hurt you. But sometimes, the things He asks us to do are uncomfortable. We may not understand exactly what is going on at the time, but if we can remember that He is the potter and we are the clay[33], it will help us get through those times. Let's take a closer look at the WORD on this subject:

> *⁴ And the vessel that he made of clay was marred in the hand of the potter; so he made it again into another vessel, as it seemed good to the potter to make.*

---

[33] Isaiah 64:8; Jeremiah 18:1-4; Romans 9:20-21

Chapter 2: God's Idea of Faithfulness

> *⁵ Then the word of the LORD came to me, saying:* *⁶ "O house of Israel,* ***can I not do with you as this potter?*** *" says the LORD. "Look, as the clay is in the potter's hand, so are you in My hand, O house of Israel!"* *(Jeremiah 18:4-6 NKJV)*

We see here that God was talking through the prophet to the House of Israel. There is something here I want to make sure everyone sees. The potter was making something, but as he worked, he saw something about it that wasn't quite right. So he basically redid it. When he finished, he decided that was really what he was after in the first place. Then, in verse 6, the LORD said to the man of God, "Tell the House of Israel, I can do with you just like this potter did with the clay."

Paul also mentions this in Romans 9:

> *²¹ Does not the potter have power over the clay, from the same lump to make one vessel for honor and another for dishonor? (Romans 9:21 NKJV)*

In the King James, that sounds like God is making one good and one bad. But other translations help us to better understand what He meant here.

> *Isn't it obvious that a potter has a perfect right to shape one lump of clay into a vase for holding flowers and another into a pot for cooking beans? (Romans 9:21b MSG)*

That's really what it says. I didn't make that up. I love that! Remember Romans 8:14 tells us, "Those who are led by the Spirit of God are the sons and daughters of God." So, no matter whether the Father made you a vase for holding flowers or a pot for cooking beans, you can trust Him, through the Holy Spirit, to lead you in the way you should go to fulfill that purpose.

So right now tell yourself, "He is the potter and I'm the clay. God's talking to me right now!" Amen! What is He molding and shaping you for? I really don't know. You will know. I don't know everything that is coming down the road, but I do know that He is shaping us and molding us. We want to be the right vessels when He's finished with us. We don't want to be teapots if He wants us to be a plate. He's the potter; it is His choice.

UNDERSTANDING GOD'S ORDER

God likes things to be done in an orderly and systematic fashion. How do we know this? Take a close look at the natural world. Almost everything in it is built in an orderly fashion with smaller pieces fitting beautifully together to make larger ones. But we also know, because He has told us in His WORD, that He is not the author of confusion and chaos, but of order and peace in which each joint fits together perfectly and supplies its part to build line upon line[34]. Therefore, God is going to move and deal with things through the order He set up.

In the local church, the pastoral office is the highest office So, that will be the office that God talks to first. In the home, while the husband and wife should both be hearing from heaven, the highest office is the husband[35]. Of course, if you are single, then God will talk to you directly.

Let me give you an example from 2 Kings to explain what I mean. Remember when Elisha was walking with Elijah. When they got to Bethel where a school for prophets was located, some of those student prophets started telling Elisha, "Do you know the LORD is going to take your master away from you today?"

Elisha gave them an interesting answer: "Yes, I know it. Hold your peace." Then the same thing happened again when they reached Jericho just before crossing the River Jordan.

Do you know why they couldn't say anything about it? They didn't qualify to speak it. They picked it up because they had the same Holy Ghost, but they didn't qualify to share it. Why not? Because it needed to go through the pastoral office over Elisha[36].

---

[34] 1 Corinthians 14:33, 40; Ephesians 4:16; Isaiah 28:10

[35] Now I know there are some ladies who are married to some men who aren't saved or aren't serving God. Please understand I am not saying that you cannot hear from God. You most definitely can, because you have the same Holy Ghost inside you.

[36] 2 Kings 2:1-9

When God has a plan for a specific local church to fulfill, He will convey that plan to the pastors of that church. They will then share it with those who have been found faithful so the plan can be carried out.

So if God is going to open doors for you, who is He going to talk to? The pastoral office. Now God will confirm some things with you and you'll have an inkling something is coming. This is why people are often confused about someone's multiple promotions. They don't understand that God has found that person faithful and is telling the pastor to promote them to positions of increased responsibility.

THE NATURAL IS THE TRAINING GROUND FOR THE SUPERNATURAL

Faithfulness isn't just about becoming the man or woman God wants us to be. It is about taking care to follow through on everything God has in His heart for us. That means being humble enough to start out small and to pay close attention to the specific details He gives. In other words, our hearts have to be in the right place.

If you've read the stories about the Exodus and the building of the Ark of the Covenant and the Tabernacle, then you remember that each item was made to exact specifications and had a specific use and place. Why? Because God said so. Think about it this way: When you and I get to glory, there won't be trash on those streets of gold. The shrubbery and flowerbeds out in front of the House of God aren't going to look a mess. God is a God of order, not chaos[37]. Keeping our natural things nice here on Earth is preparation for the order and beauty of heaven.

It's the same for the physical House of God here. Have you ever walked into a church sanctuary for a Sunday morning service and the chairs have all been a crazy mess? Of course not! If there was a Holy Ghost meeting, then they ought to be torn up from the floor at the end of the service, but not at the beginning. When people walk into a church, they expect to see the chairs in some sort of an orderly arrangement.

---

[37] 1 Corinthians 14:33

In preparation for the service, the pastor may ask you to move the chairs, vacuum under them, and then put them back in, let's say, a half-moon shape. They want it exactly the way they said. Yet, all of us have flesh. When someone tells us to do something, most of us feel that flesh rise up and growl from time to time. Ephesians 2:2 tells us that is a spirit of disobedience. In other words, something from the spirit realm is trying to influence us.

Therefore, we must be quick to obey willingly and accurately. We must learn to put that thing under our feet and take those thoughts captive. It is easy to understand that when you are vacuuming the sanctuary and lining up those chairs, you are doing something in the natural. But do you realize the spiritual always touches the natural? Why? Because the natural is the training ground for the supernatural. We have to get it right in the natural if we want to receive more of the supernatural.

FAITHFULNESS IS THE KEY TO PROMOTION

It amazes me how God will pick someone out of a crowd and give them an assignment, and people wonder, "Well, how come they get to do that?" Simple, it was God's choosing. But it wasn't on God's side only. The man or the woman He chose had a lot to do with it because they were willing to do what He asked. Faithfulness is the key to opening that door.

It is exhausting to deal with someone who wants to argue or complain about everything. I'm not saying God gets tired, but I am saying it is a whole lot better when a person is willing to do whatever God asks without arguing, complaining, or debating.

We've all been a kid and many of us have kids so let me use kids to illustrate what I mean. My wife and I have a wealth of kids. In other words, we have a lot. Some are ours, some are adopted, and some just lived with us and we claim them as ours. We never let them try to negotiate with us about church. It didn't matter how late they were out on a Saturday night, church the next morning was non-negotiable. We never let our kids ask "Why?" either. We just had too many of them to let them do that. Sally and I weren't about to sit around all day and explain over and over again why they had to do something. So when they asked, we

Chapter 2: God's Idea of Faithfulness

just said, "Because I told you to do it. Now if you don't want to do it, let me whip on you a little bit and then you'll do it. So you go on and do your crying, and when I get back, I expect that to be done."

Now let's look at a more spiritual example. Pastor John could be having his quiet time with the LORD. When the LORD says, "You know, Brother Jimmy has been faithful. He has been helping and he's been doing everything I ask to take care of you. He picks up your car and washes it and does several other things for Me. I want you to bring him up in the Helps Ministry concerning this certain area." That wasn't Pastor John's idea; it was God's. Faithfulness will always bring you up before God[38].

But sometimes, people want to think the pastor just has favorites. No, that's not it. We operate just like everyone else—by the leading of the inward witness. If God speaks something to us as leaders about someone, then it's not because of favoritism. It's because God knows their heart, and knows they are willing to obey Him. God is just like any other employer. He doesn't want somebody on the job who's going to fight Him all the time. He wants somebody who is going to do it the way He says and when He says to do it. In his book *Jesus the Open Door*, Brother Hagin said, *"Whatever small door He opens for you, walk through it"* (p. 83). I would add to that statement that you should be faithful there and keep studying the WORD so He can open bigger doors of service for you.

A few pages later in the same book, Brother Hagin wrote:

> *"The point is that God richly blesses **obedience**—no matter where you serve Him! God will richly reward you as you walk through the door of service He has opened for **you**"* (p. 90).

In Galatians 5 of the King James Translation, faith is listed as a fruit of the Spirit. However, more modern translations have a word that is closer to the original: faithfulness. We know how faith comes—*by hearing, and hearing by the WORD of God*[39]. So it isn't faith that is a fruit of the Spirit. It is faithfulness which must be developed over time in a relationship with

---

[38] Acts 10:4, 31
[39] Romans 10:17

God. When people are coming up in the ranks, so to speak, it isn't because the pastor prefers them. It is because God has found them faithful. By the same token, if you are not moving and want to, you better start inventorying your life to see what's in your heart, and if you are faithful according to God's definition of the word. God isn't looking for superstars. He is looking for people He can make into stars—faithful people. What do you want to hear your Father say when you stand before Him? We all want to hear, "Well done! Enter in to the joy of the Lord[40]."

---

[40] Matthew 25:21

CHAPTER 3 – EXAMPLES OF FAITHFULNESS

THE UNFAITHFUL KING

Saul was the first king of Israel. The Bible records that he was tall and handsome and the people were very pleased to have him as their leader. But when it was time for him to be crowned, the people could not find him because he was hiding among the equipment[41]. He sounds like a lot of people I know when God asks them to do something. There was an open door of opportunity right before him, and, at least at first, he wasn't really sure if he trusted God enough to go on through it. Of course, we know he did go on to become king. Let's look at how this played out for Saul:

> *[21] And afterward they desired a king: and God gave unto them Saul the son of Cis, a man of the tribe of Benjamin, by the space of **forty years**. [22] **And when he had removed him**, he raised up unto them David to be their king; to whom also he gave their testimony, and said, I have found David the son of Jesse, a man after mine own heart, which shall fulfill all my will. (Acts 13:21-22 KJV)*

So how long was Saul king? Forty years. Now look at the first phrase of verse 22: *"And when he had removed him…"* That sounds like a closed door, doesn't it[42]? What happened? If you have a reference Bible, it will point you to all the events that led up to this. Specifically, let's look at 1 Samuel 15 where God gave Saul some very specific instructions through the prophet Samuel:

> *[1] Samuel said to Saul, "I am the one the LORD sent to anoint you king over his people Israel; so listen now to the message from the LORD. [2] This is what the LORD Almighty*

---

[41] 1 Samuel 10:17-27
[42] More about open and closed doors in Part 2.

> says: 'I will punish the Amalekites for what they did to Israel when they waylaid them as they came up from Egypt. ³ Now go, attack the Amalekites, and totally destroy all that belongs to them. Do not spare them; put to death men and women, children and infants, cattle and sheep, camels and donkeys.'" (1 Kings 15:1-3 NKJV)

Those were some very specific instructions, or steps, to follow for that war:

1. Attack the Amalekites
2. Totally destroy all that belongs to them
3. Put to death all the men, women, children, and infants
4. Kill the cattle, sheep, camels, and donkeys

He was to annihilate everything that had to do with the Amalekites[43]. He wasn't to leave anything breathing. Nothing.

Now, focusing on faithfulness, we see in verse 7 that Saul showed up, and he went to war. Many have struggled with this passage because they have confused Saul's going to war with faithfulness. They think just because he showed up, he was faithful. But to determine if he was faithful, we must look at whether he followed God's specific instructions.

> ⁷ Then Saul attacked the Amalekites all the way from Havilah to Shur, near the eastern border of Egypt. ⁸ He took Agag king of the Amalekites alive, and all his people he totally destroyed with the sword. ⁹ But Saul and the army spared Agag and the best of the sheep and cattle, the fat calves and lambs—everything that was good. These they were unwilling to destroy completely, but everything that was despised and weak they totally destroyed. (1 Samuel 15:7 NKJV)

Let's jump ahead a bit to get more information about the situation with King Saul:

---

[43] Deuteronomy 32:35; Romans 12:19

Chapter 3: Examples of Faithfulness

> *¹³ And Samuel came to Saul: and Saul said unto him, Blessed be thou of the LORD: I have performed the commandment of the LORD.*
>
> *¹⁴ And Samuel said, What meaneth then this bleating of the sheep in mine ears, and the lowing of the oxen which I hear?*
>
> *¹⁵ And Saul said, They have brought them from the Amalekites: for the people spared the best of the sheep and of the oxen, to sacrifice unto the LORD thy God; and the rest we have utterly destroyed. (1 Samuel 15:13-15 KJV)*

Now, what was in God's heart? He said, "Don't keep anything." We all know there were other times in the Bible where God said to go ahead and keep the spoils. But what is in God's heart right now for this situation? "Don't keep any of it." So, what actions qualified as faithfulness in this situation? Executing the plan—destroying everything and everyone—without adding to or taking away from it.

We're talking about trusting God and faithfully executing what He said in the way He said to do it. Clearly, Saul didn't do that. He even kept King Agag alive as a prisoner of war. Saul wanted to parade him up and down in his victory parade when he went home. But Samuel told him, "You haven't obeyed God. Is sacrificing an offering better than obedience?" *(verse 22)*.

God didn't want the Amalekites' animals as sacrifices. He wanted Saul to obey faithfully. But Saul wanted to push it off and say, "Well, I showed up and went to war. So I ought to get some credit for that" *(verses 20-21)*. But he didn't get it, because he didn't do what God said to do, and what he did do wasn't what was in God's heart. This was a test of faithfulness and Saul failed, but it wasn't the only time God tested him. There were many tests and many failures.

> *²² **And when he had removed him**, he raised up unto them David to be their king; to whom also he gave their testimony, and said, I have found David the son of Jesse, a*

> *man after mine own heart, which shall fulfil all my will. (Acts 13:22 KJV)*

> *¹³ So **Saul died because he was unfaithful to the LORD**. He failed to obey the LORD's command, and he even consulted a **medium**⁴⁴. (1 Chronicles 10:13 NLT, footnote mine)*

It says in 1 Chronicles 10:13 that Saul died because *he was unfaithful to the LORD*. How was Saul *unfaithful*? He didn't complete all the steps God gave him. He added to the instructions he was given. He kept the best animals and paraded the king around downtown to show off. Since this wasn't what God had in His heart for Saul to do, He considered Saul's actions unfaithful and closed the door on his time as king of Israel. Eventually, Saul's unfaithfulness and disobedience cost him everything—not just the kingdom, but his life and the life of his son, Jonathan, as well.

Some wonder if Saul disobeyed because he didn't understand *why* God wanted the Amalekites utterly destroyed⁴⁵. Saul was in the same boat as Noah a few thousand years earlier. There were several things God told Noah to do where He didn't explain everything. For example, do you remember the giant door on that boat? There was no way for Noah to close it, yet he didn't tamper with the design. He made it just the way God said. In the end, it didn't matter if King Saul understood the why, as long as he understood the order came directly from God. Remember, when this all wraps up, we are accountable to God and no one else⁴⁶. Saul's disobedience revealed his true heart towards God.

---

⁴⁴ A medium is a go-between or intermediary (Medium). In this case, the intermediary was between the natural realm and the spirit realm when Saul used the witch at Endor to call up the spirit of Samuel from the dead and ask him about the looming battle with the Philistines because God would no longer speak to him (1 Samuel 28).

⁴⁵ The Bible doesn't tell us why God wanted them destroyed. It is His prerogative *not* to tell us. We understand their history of idolatry, and how they treated people—especially God's people—probably had something to do with it.

⁴⁶ Hebrews 4:13

Chapter 3: Examples of Faithfulness

THE FAITHFUL BOY

Now, let's turn our attention from the unfaithful first king of Israel to the faithful second king.

> *²² And when he had removed him, he raised up unto them David to be their king; to whom also he gave their testimony, and said, I have found **David** the son of Jesse, **a man after mine own heart, which shall fulfill all my will.** (Acts 13:22 KJV)*

There was quite a gap of time from the point when God decided to remove the first king and the installation of the second king. In the meantime, the young boy, who would become king, had to continue in faithful service to God, to his family, and to his king after his anointing until the time came to take the throne.

I love the story of David's anointing as the future king of Israel in 1 Samuel 16. Samuel had been mourning over Saul's unfaithfulness and fall from grace. God told him to get up and go to Jesse's house to offer a sacrifice and to anoint the future king. Well, when Samuel arrived, Jesse lined up all his boys except David, because he was the youngest and out in the fields tending the sheep. Jesse apparently didn't bother bringing him in because he considered him entirely too young for consideration. Samuel was sure it would be the first one, Eliab, because he was tall and good-looking. But notice what God said:

> *⁶ When they arrived, Samuel took one look at Eliab and thought, "Surely this is the LORD's anointed!"*
>
> *⁷ But the LORD said to Samuel, "Don't judge by his appearance or height, for I have rejected him. The LORD doesn't see things the way you see them. People judge by outward appearance, but **the LORD looks at the heart.**" (1 Samuel 16:6-7 NLT)*

God's response shows us that faithfulness is a heart issue. Saul had a problem submitting to authority. Once that door shut for Saul, no one could open it, not even Samuel. Because it isn't about leadings or showing up, it is about faithfulness.

Faithfulness

Each of Jesse's sons walked past Samuel, but God rejected them all. Eventually, Samuel realized something was wrong and asked Jesse if he had another son. Remember, Jesse had incorrectly assumed there was no way God would anoint David because of his youth. After Samuel asked about another son, Jesse sent for him. Samuel finally anointed young David. They had a feast, and life returned to normal. The future king went back to faithfully tending the sheep[47].

Remember how God told Samuel that He looks at the heart? We cannot see what is in someone's heart, but God can. This is not just something tacked onto the story. It is an important fact and a clue to something in the heart of Eliab and the other brothers. Nothing else is said about this brother, Eliab, until later in chapter 17. At that point, Jesse's oldest sons are out on the hillside with Israel's army. David was still young and still tending the sheep for his dad. One day, Jesse sent David to take some food to his brothers. On the way, David started asking the men what was going on. Look what Eliab said when he saw David:

> [28] *And Eliab his eldest brother heard when he spake unto the men; and Eliab's anger was kindled against David, and he said, Why camest thou down hither? and with whom hast thou left those few sheep in the wilderness?* ***I know thy pride, and the naughtiness of thine heart****; for thou art come down that thou mightest see the battle. (1 Samuel 17:28 KJV)*

Eliab was being very rude and accusing David of some heart issues. At the same time, we can clearly see that Eliab did not have the boldness to trust God, because he was hiding behind a rock. Samuel and Jesse, as men, would not have known this was in his heart the day Samuel came to anoint the future king. Like most of us, Eliab had the ability to bury it and hide it under a façade of politeness. But God knew. David, on the other hand, didn't even really care what Eliab said, because someone had already told him the one who slew the giant would get the king's daughter as a wife.

---

[47] 1 Samuel 16:10-13

Chapter 3: Examples of Faithfulness

He didn't hesitate when he heard Goliath slandering Israel. He walked right up to Saul and offered to be God's man to kill Goliath *(verse 32)*.

Just like Abraham, it took some time for David to develop that kind of trust in God. Right after he said he would kill Goliath, he began to rehearse some of the testimonies of how God had delivered him in the past. But King Saul was skeptical. He reminded David that Goliath had been training for war since he was a kid. King Saul stressed how big Goliath was and how he was a well-trained man of war *(verse 33)*. But David's faith wasn't shaken. He just told King Saul about the time he was out on a hill strumming a harp and worshiping when the power of God came on him and a lion snuck up at the same time. I imagine that story went something like this:

"I was just strumming along on my harp and worshiping God. Now I wasn't so overtaken that I wasn't aware of my surroundings, because I heard a sheep screaming, 'Bah, bah, bah!' So I looked up and saw that baby lamb lying in the mouth of a big old lion. As the lion took off running, that lamb was just a bleating, 'Help, David, help!' In a heartbeat, I took off after that lion and grabbed its tail."

Now the Bible tells us that David wasn't a big guy, so I'm sure he went dirt skiing with that lion for a while. Think about this: Lions weigh 3 or 400 pounds[48], and here's little ol' 100-pound David hanging on back there. Even if David weighed 150, that ain't no match! The lamb is dangling out of the lion's mouth and David's got the lion by the tail and he's dirt skiing. Finally, the lion probably looked around and thought, "Are you kidding me? You're a human. I'm a lion. I'm king of the beasts."

David would continue on, "Eventually, the lion let go of the lamb, so he could go for me! I wasn't worried though, because I had been strumming on my harp and had found out about my weapon of praise. So I just told him, 'I was going to let you go, Mr. Lion, but you came after me.' Then, I grabbed that lion's beard and snapped his jaw. Whack! Pow!!"

---

[48] Asiatic lions, which are slightly smaller and have smaller manes than their African cousins, most likely roamed Israel during David's time, although they are found only in one forest in India now. For more information on lions in the Bible visit http://www.bible-history.com/links.php?cat=41&sub=802.

As David related this story to King Saul, I'm pretty sure the king said something like, "Really? You? Let me see you flex your muscles, Boy!"

But David didn't stop there. He went on to tell about another time when he was playing his flute and a bear[49] got one of his lambs. You can bet he wasn't singing that *Wizard of Oz*[50] song, "Lions and Tigers and Bears, Oh My!" No! He was singing praises to his King! He went down and grabbed that bear and took the lamb right out of its mouth.

Now after rehearsing both of those stories, young David's faith fire was stoked and built up, so he started shouting, "Who does this uncircumcised Philistine think he is? Because God Almighty has delivered him into our hands" *(verses 33-37)*. This boy was raring to go with God and get the victory just like Joshua and Caleb[51].

But King Saul was focused only on what he could do in the natural. He wanted to protect David, so he told David to wear his armor *(verse 38)*. I can see it now.

David put it all on. But since he was so small and King Saul was so tall, it swallowed him up. So he said, "Sir, thank you for the thought, but I haven't proven this."

David needed armor and weapons he had proven in which he could trust. So he went on, "But there's something I have proven, and that's Jehovah! This is something I've tried and it's the name of Jesus! This is something that I know works! It's called trust in God! Thank you for the thought, but if you don't mind, I'll go with what I'm familiar with—the WORD—the anointing! I'll go get your giant!"

Of course, you know the story. He took off all that heavy armor and boldly, with no fear, he walked down off the side of that hill and down into that stream to pick up five smooth stones. But one was all it took.

---

[49] According to www.bearsoftheworld.net, the Syrian brown bear was once natural to Israel, but is no longer. For more information on bears in the Bible, visit http://www.bible-history.com/links.php?cat=41&sub=818.

[50] *The Wizard of Oz* is a popular American movie released in 1939, based on a series of children's books by L. Frank Baum, in which Dorothy and her little dog, Toto, get caught up in a tornado and end up in the magical land of Oz where they have all sorts of heroic adventures.

[51] Numbers 13:30; 14:6-9, 24

Chapter 3: Examples of Faithfulness

Hallelujah! By recounting those stories to King Saul, the boy built up his faith in God to the point that nothing was going to stop him. This pleased God because David believed He existed and believed that God would reward him for his faithfulness[52].

In Acts 13 God said, "I have found a man that will do it the way I have it in my heart" *(verse 22)!* Remember, David's brother, Eliab, with the heart issues? We left him hiding behind a rock in fear. God doesn't want people cowering behind rocks. He wants somebody like David who isn't afraid to stand up to the devil and tell him to shut his mouth. He wants somebody to stand in front of cancer to curse it and command it to die and come out of a body.

David killed the lion, he killed the bear, and he killed the giant. And because he took God at His WORD, God promised David that the entire world throughout all generations would know this story[53]. That promise has been fulfilled. I don't care who they are, they know about David and Goliath. God called him faithful.

Let's look at Acts 13:22 again in a couple of translations, because I really want to make sure we understand what God is saying:

> *[22] But God removed Saul and replaced him with David, a man about whom God said, 'I have found David son of Jesse, a man after my own heart.* **He will do everything I want him to do.**' *(Acts 13:22 NLTe)*

> *[20-22] "Up to the time of Samuel the prophet, God provided judges to lead them. But then they asked for a king, and God gave them Saul, son of Kish, out of the tribe of Benjamin. After Saul had ruled forty years, God removed him from office and put King David in his place, with this commendation: 'I've searched the land and found this David, son of Jesse.* **He's a man whose heart beats to my**

---

[52] Hebrews 11:6
[53] 2 Samuel 7:8-16

heart, a man who will do what I tell him.'" *(Acts 13:20-22 MSG)*

----

²² And when He had deposed him, He raised up David to be their king; of him He bore witness and said, I have found David son of Jesse a man after My own heart, **who will do all My will** *and* **carry out My program fully***. (Acts 13:22 AMPC)*

First Samuel 2:35 says the same thing. God knew David would do what was in His heart, not what was in David's own heart.

For years, I thought the reason God said that David was *a man after His own heart* was because David was quick to repent and quick to forgive. Both are very good qualities and we should all have them in our lives. But we see here, God saw so much more in David, as He does in us. He saw a man who would *carry out His program fully*—every step with nothing missing and nothing broken. David wanted to do what God had in His heart—the way God had it decided. In other words, he made up his mind that he wasn't going to alter the plan God gave him. Whatever God told him to do, he was going to do it exactly that way whether he fully understood the reasoning behind the instruction or not.

This encompasses more than just diligently showing up every day in the meadow with the sheep or in the throne room with the subjects. In fact, the Common English Bible translates this verse in such a way to say that David shared the same desires as God (Acts 13:22 (CEB)). Isn't that interesting? God says right here that faithfulness is doing everything He has in His heart, not just showing up and being diligent. Diligence and hard work are good, but they don't encompass the whole plan of faithfulness.

There is more to this verse I want to make sure you see which isn't always easy to see in the current English translations. God was excited to find David.

*²² God removed Saul and made David their king. God spoke favorably about David. He said, '****I have found that***

Chapter 3: Examples of Faithfulness

***David**, son of Jesse, is a man after my own heart. **He will do everything I want him to do.**' (Acts 13:22 God's Word)*

Some older translations say, "I have found a man!" They translate it as though God is jumping up and down with excitement because He had searched for so long. But then He found David and He called him faithful, because he would do *everything* God wanted him to do immediately, boldly, and without fear.

As I was studying this, I was surprised to find that God got excited about David. He's like, "Woo-hoo! Looky here! I've found a man!"

I'm thinking, "Good Lord, there had to have been at least several hundred thousand people on Earth at that time." Yet to me it looks like He's excited that He's found *one*. It reminded me of the first part of 2 Chronicles 16:9, *"For the eyes of the LORD run to and fro throughout the whole earth, to shew himself strong in the behalf of them whose heart is perfect toward him" (KJV)*. In other words, He's always looking for somebody who will do it the way He has it in His heart that He might do exploits through them.

Isn't that wonderful? That's why when I get before Jesus, I don't want Him to look at me and ask, "Well?" No! I want Him to say, "Well done thou good and *faithful* servant – the one who trusted Me and did it the way I had it in my heart" *(Matthew 25:21)*.

Now it is your turn. Say out loud, "I'm glad I'm faithful. Whenever God tells me to do something, I will do it the way He says. I will do it the way He has it in His heart. I'll do it immediately, boldly, and without fear."

OUR OWN FAITHFULNESS JOURNEY

In 1986, we headed to Bible school at Rhema Bible Training Center (Rhema) in Broken Arrow, Oklahoma, and graduated two years later in 1988. Graduation was at the end of May, and then we went to southeast Texas to spend a month with my wife's folks. We had been busy in school and working, so they hadn't seen the grandkids for two full years. At this same time, a church in southern Oklahoma offered us a position. They also offered to buy us an evangelism tent, because I thought I was the next R.W. Schambach[54]. I did. God help us all!

In time, however, we settled in Silsbee, Texas. We attended a little prayer group there for a long time. They kept asking us to pastor them, but I kept turning them down and telling them that I was an evangelist. In my mind, I was saying, "I'm the next R.W. Schambach. But thank-you." So we just kept traveling around preaching for a while and would not accept a pastorate anywhere.

Eventually, God woke us up early one morning with some Scripture and told us that we were called to pastor that little flock. We took the pastorate and that little prayer group became a local church. But we still wouldn't buy a house. We just kept telling ourselves we were only going to be here for a little while because we were really called to itinerant ministry. It took us three years to figure out we might be here a little while, and we should buy a house.

Of course, we loved those people and we loved that place. When we started in that little church, there were times that it would just be me, my wife, and maybe one other couple. Sometimes it was just us. That's when you truly learn the meaning of "the more you give, the more you receive[55]!" Amen! When you are the only ones giving, if you don't give, then there ain't nothing for salary.

It was a fun little place. We were in a little 20' x 20' portable building. I had a tiny little wood pulpit at the front and we could crowd in about 20 people on little metal chairs. The bathroom was right beside the pulpit with a door that swung toward the wall, so you could see right in to the toilet. Many times, I'd be preaching along, and some little kid would open the door and holler, "Momma, wipe me!" Thank God for small beginnings. Amen! Hallelujah! It was just wild!

We went from there to the M&M Grocery Store. It was an old building, so it had metal poles down right down the middle. We trained

---

[54] Rev. R.W. Schambach entered the ministry after serving in World War 2. He was an anointed evangelist well-known for his tent crusades. You can read more about him and his ministry at http://schambachfoundation.org/legacy/

[55] Luke 6:38

everybody that when the power of God came on them to run on the right side of the poles and to always keep their eyes OPEN. Otherwise, they might run smack into a pole! Amen! If somebody hit one of those poles, they'd end up with a knot big enough for a calf to suck. Boing! That baby would knock them smooth out and it wouldn't be by the unction either!

After the grocery store, we ended up moving to a Mexican restaurant. It was painted that real brilliant pink you see them in so often, with a great big black toro bull painted on the outside wall. He had his head down and tail up, ready for a fight. The church board came to me and wanted to get rid him quick as lightning. But I told them, "Oh no, I'm going to write above it, 'Jesus loves you! No bull!'" We had such a good time there.

Eventually, we bought a building of our own. So you can see, we had been through a lot with this group of people. Those kinds of bonds are not easily broken. Yet, several years later in 1996, we began to sense that change was coming. We weren't sure on the specifics. And most of you know that change can represent a lot of things. Well, we didn't know what the change was, but God said if we would be faithful to go through the door He was opening for us, it would bring a great increase.

A few weeks later, we were in some meetings in Beaumont, Texas, with Dick Mills[56]. Sure enough, he called us out in that meeting and confirmed that change was coming. He began to tell us that "the Spirit of God would come upon us and we would be changed to another man[57]," and different things along those lines. This was a confirmation of the stirring from the inward witness. Now we knew for sure that change was coming, but we still didn't understand the details of it. We still didn't know what kind of change to expect.

---

[56] Dick Mills was an amazing and anointed man of God who contributed the "Word Wealth" New Testament portion of the *Spirit-Filled Believer's Bible*, published by Thomas Nelson Publishers (Dick Mills Ministries). Reverend Mills operated in the gifts of the Spirit in an unusual way. He would call someone out and give them Scripture. Then he would prophesy things to them and explain the things God was saying. He always used a Scripture, and he could quote almost every translation there was. It was a very unique gifting. He was the only man I've ever seen do that.

[57] 1 Samuel 10:6

Then over a period of time, it began to get a little difficult for us at the church. The people weren't difficult. They still loved us. It had to do with my wife and me, and it was critical that we didn't let that frustration during our waiting time affect our ability to minister to other people. Just because things were changing, and weren't like they used to be in our hearts, didn't mean they had changed in anyone else's.

We still had an assignment to complete there. We still had to be kind and pastor that church and minister to that flock the best we could until God said, "Okay, I've got a new shepherd coming for them and here's where you go now." This is a trap that many people fall into whether they are leaders or not. God gives them a warning that change is coming, and they want to jump out ahead of Him before their current assignment is completed. We cannot allow frustration to sway faithfulness, because faithfulness always sees the assignment all the way to completion.

Eventually, it was clear to us that it was time to leave Silsbee. God sent us back to Oklahoma. We stayed with family for a while and planned to travel full-time as itinerant ministers. You see, during the previous seven years, I had been preaching between nine to eleven times a week, because we were on the radio, and had helped to start some other works. We did all this while still having small children at home.

Our lives had been very busy, and, truth be told, by this point I was tired. So, I asked the LORD for some time off when we made this move to Oklahoma. I told Him I wanted to spend some time with the kids, and then I would go preach as much as He wanted and anywhere He wanted. God is so good and so generous! He gave me three months off! But He made it very clear that I was going back to work after that.

I did exactly as He instructed. Then that fall—even though I already had meetings booked up in Washington, Oregon, and the Northwest—the LORD said, "I want you to start a work in Pawnee."

"What?" I asked shocked. "LORD, I thought we were just going to travel full-time?" Very often, we think we know what the plan is, but we really don't. God is so much smarter than us. He won't tell us everything. He knows better because most of the time if He did we'd quit!

Chapter 3: Examples of Faithfulness

So I called my wife and discussed it with her. She told me she thought it was God. We agreed we would do it. But we didn't do it right away. I kept traveling. This eventually became a problem because two years had passed since God gave us the prophetic word that change was coming. This new work was the change He was talking about. So it was time to get after the plan.

Finally, in February 1998, we started a church in a garage and kept going. Now we had the church at home in Pawnee where we pastored together, and I was still traveling around preaching part-time. It was another very busy season.

As time passed, I could tell there was something else coming on, but I wasn't sure what. Eventually, God explained to me, "Sally is supposed to be the pastor here, and you're going to start traveling full-time again."

So I went to my wife and told her, "Honey, you're the pastor here and God wants me to travel."

She said, "Oh, Honey, no. I don't think men will receive from me because I'm a woman." I reassured her that they would, and I would help her. But she just didn't want to do it. You see this is a good work. We have as many men as we do women. We have a good mix of young and older men.

Well, one day we were in a meeting with Dr. Ed Dufresne, who became our spiritual father after Brother Hagin went to be with the LORD. He came by and slapped her on the head and said, "You're the pastor of the church."

She kind of shrugged and said, "Okay."

I'm sitting there thinking, "Really? Okay, fine."

After the meeting, I said, "I told you that, and you wouldn't do it. But Dad Dufresne tells you and you're all for it?" We had a good laugh and she willingly stepped into her new role.

Sally is a wonderful lady and a wonderful wife, but she felt like she needed some transitioning time. You see, she had always helped with the ministry, but had never pastored full-time. We discussed it and concluded we would need two or three years to complete the transition.

So I went to God to discuss it with Him. I asked, "God, would You please give us two years. I'm not being rebellious, Sir, she needs help to turn the ship. I'd like to be close to the church for the next two years, and then I'll get after my part again." He said that was fine. Over the next two years, we transitioned to her doing the preaching and me being there showing that I supported her, and we turned that ship. Now, she is a preaching machine!

Every time God gives you an instruction, whether He qualifies your obedience as faithful or not, depends on how quickly you do it and how closely you obey the exact instruction given to you. Quick and close obedience always qualifies as faithfulness. At each point, we could have kept on just as we were and told ourselves that we were doing something great. But no matter what we told ourselves, we would not have been considered faithful in God's eyes.

CHAPTER 4 – FAITHFULNESS REQUIRES TRUST

Over the years, I have learned that God doesn't have to explain Himself to me. Have you noticed that too? If He chooses to, He will. But if not, I mean to tell you, He can be as silent as the grave. I have bugged Him about some stuff and He wouldn't say a word. He just wouldn't! Sometimes, He'd tell me to go do something and I would ask Him, "Well, uh, how come?" or, I would be like Peter and ask, "What about John[58]?" or "What about Pastor Boudreaux? Why me?" and He wouldn't say a thing! He'd just clam up! You see, trusting God means we are faithful even when we don't fully understand why He has asked us to do something or what the next step is going to be after this one.

ABRAHAM TRUSTED GOD

Let's explore the role of trust in Abraham's faithfulness to God. I've already mentioned that God found Abraham faithful. He tested Abraham many times over the course of his lifetime. Probably, the most famous test was asking him to sacrifice Isaac. Yet, when God first introduced Himself to Abraham (then called Abram), there was no way that He could ask him to sacrifice his son. Abram just didn't have enough experience with God to know if he could trust Him that far yet. In fact, it would be decades before he would even be able to trust God for Baby Isaac in the first place. But Abram did trust God when He asked him to leave his homeland and his kinfolk[59].

As I've studied the Scriptures and spent time with the LORD, I've learned that faithfulness actually means trusting God enough to do what He asks, exactly the way He asks, and the way He has it in His heart. Once

---
[58] Remember Peter in John 21:21.
[59] Genesis 11:30–12:4.

we understand this, we can understand why God would repeatedly test Abraham. Over time, as Abraham took each step and completed each task God asked him to do, he saw that he could trust God, even to the point of sacrificing his beloved Isaac. Eventually, God called Abraham faithful, but there were many tests between Genesis 12 and Hebrews 11.

> *⁹ So then they which be of **faith** are **blessed** with **faithful Abraham**. (Galatians 3:9 KJV)*

There are two things I'd like you to make note of here. First, Abraham had faith in God, meaning Abraham learned to trust God. Second, God trusted Abraham. How do we know this? God called Abraham faithful. You don't call someone faithful if you don't trust them. Let's look at trusting God first.

> *"**God** is **not a man, that He should lie**, Nor a son of man, that He should repent. Has He said, and will He not do? Or has He spoken, and will He not make it good?" (Numbers 23:19 NKJV)*

God told us that He isn't a man and doesn't lie so we will trust Him. We can all think of times a person has abused our trust and hurt us. But God isn't a man. When things don't happen with people the way you expect them to, don't fall out with God. You can still trust Him no matter what it looks like with people.

God showed me the importance of this on more than one occasion. In fact, in 1985 my wife and I had our first home together. Just as it was almost paid off, God began to deal with us to leave it and go to school at Rhema.

The Jewish man who financed it for us came to America as a small child, then he was sent to our area on one of the orphan trains. When he got here, he didn't even have a name, just a little tag wrapped around his neck. He had worked very hard all his life and was a very wealthy man. But now, he and his wife were in their 70s and found themselves with no children. Since he liked my wife and me so much, he sold us a home with a bunch of land.

However, he had an unusual provision in the contract with us. It said that if we left before paying it off, he could choose to take it all back. In that case, we'd forfeit everything we had paid. Sure enough, when I told him we were leaving, he became very upset and said, "I want to take everything back." Keep in mind, we lacked only a few months and it would have been all ours. This was very painful for me. I tell you what, I cried and was an emotional wreck for quite a while.

Then the LORD began to talk to me and asked, "Why are you so upset?" Now here is something that is so precious about the LORD: He will meet you wherever you are. And, no matter where we are, God is always even bigger. He went on to ask me another question, "Do you understand why you are so emotionally torn up right now?"

I answered him honestly, "Well, it's our home. We're walking away from all this and it's almost paid for."

He gently responded, "No. That's really not it. You haven't walked with Me long enough yet to really know that you can trust Me. You are upset because you don't know if you'll ever have another home that is paid for. You just haven't been with Me long enough. Son, I'm telling you, you can trust Me, but it takes time and progression."

You see, we must learn to trust Him with our day-to-day lives, not just our eternity. Think back to the story of Abraham. What was the very first thing God asked him to do? Leave his country and his family[60]. Twenty-four *years* later[61], He asked Abraham to circumcise himself and all the males in his household[62]. Ten years after that, God asked Abraham for his son, Isaac[63]. Over the course of 34 years, a trust had developed between those two to the point that the writer of Hebrews records Abraham was so confident in God that "even if he stabbed his own son, he believed God would raise him up from the dead[64]." You just don't get to that point of confidence and trust overnight, but you can get there.

Keep in mind, trust is a two-way street. When the Bible talks about the faith of Abraham, it means that Abraham had learned to trust God. But

---

[60] Genesis 12:1
[61] Genesis 12:4; 17:24
[62] Genesis 17
[63] Genesis 22:1-17
[64] Hebrews 11:17-19

God also trusted Abraham to do what He asked when and how He asked Abraham to do it.

For example, when a husband and wife first get married, they know in a general, or theoretical, sense that they can trust their spouse. But they usually don't have a lot of specific experience trusting them. However, as they grow older together, that trust grows because of the experiences they have shared. They eventually trust each other with their lives. In that same way, there is a trust relationship that develops between you and your Father God. Let me encourage you. No matter what He asks you to do, you can trust Him. Even if it doesn't make sense at the time, later it will. Right now, it might not. But you can still trust Him.

NOAH TRUSTED GOD

Noah is another great example of this. God told him to make a boat because a flood was coming, and Noah didn't even know what a flood was[65]. God also gave him very specific directions for the ark. He told him exactly what type of wood to use and how to make the pitch. One thing was especially peculiar. God's plans called for a door that was so big there would be no way for Noah to close it. Yet, he still obeyed God and made that boat on dry ground with a giant door that he had no idea how to close. He didn't alter anything from the plan God gave him. Talk about a hard place. None of them even knew what rain was, let alone a flood or a boat. Noah never did close that door. The Bible tells us that God had to do it[66].

Growing up, I always thought the ark would've looked something like one of our ships today. However, from the illustrations I've seen as I've grown up in the LORD, it was actually more or less shaped like a rectangular box. From what I can tell, if Noah had deviated from the plan just a little bit, it probably still would have floated. But it would have revealed a heart problem to God.

---

[65] Genesis 2:5-6; Hebrews 11:7
[66] Genesis 7:16

Chapter 4: Faithfulness Requires Trust

WE TRUSTED GOD

God has told us to do some of the wildest stuff too, and He hasn't always explained to us why He wanted us to do it. Yet there was no doubt it was Him telling us because we had a witness in our heart. Every single time the results have been amazing.

For example, several years ago, I owned a very nice black Ford pick-up truck. This was a relatively new truck for me. It was two or three years old and had only about 70,000 miles on it[67]. I was driving to church on a Sunday morning when the Spirit of God spoke up and said, "Trade this one off and get another one."

Well, the first thing I did was look at the miles. Then I looked around at the interior and I thought, "Man, it still smells new in here." I started to argue with Him. "This is really a…"

But before I could finish the sentence, I heard very sternly, "JUST DO WHAT YOU WANT TO DO THEN!"

I thought, "Oh snap! I have made God mad!" I immediately repented, "I'm sorry. Father, I will do that."

So I told my wife and she helped me out by getting online to research this. She found a '08 Lincoln pick-up truck in Kansas. The guy had bought it brand-new. He completely dressed it up and reduced the price of it $25,000. It had only 1,000 miles on it. So I went and got it.

I did my best to keep that truck in tiptop shape. I took really good care of it and kept it nice. Many people have confused my care of that truck as worshiping it. But that is not the case. I took care of it because my Father God arranged for me to have it and I wanted to honor Him with it by being faithful to maintain it. Now I drove that girl hard, but I took good care of her. In fact, I drove her 180,000 miles and when I sold her, she still looked almost brand-new and ran like a champ.

Many people today want a new car, but they won't be faithful with the one they have. They don't take care of it and they won't let go of it when God tells them to; therefore, He cannot give them what they desire[68]. My

---

[67] To date we have driven 1.3 million miles for the ministry.
[68] Luke 16:9-12

vehicle is my chariot. I ride all over the United States in it. I'm faithful to God and my vehicles have been faithful to me.

We have watched God do stuff like that over the years. But the only way you can be successful with Him on these endeavors is to keep your head out of it. When He gives you something simple to do like that, do it just as quickly as you can. We've learned to pass the tests while they are easy because there is coming a day when you'll need to face a giant. Obey without delay and then He will find you faithful.

CHAPTER 5 – FAITHFULNESS REQUIRES TRAINING

DO NOT DESPISE SMALL BEGINNINGS

I was brought up in the country and was such a rough-around-the-edges cowboy that I would fight a bus off. It's just how I was raised, and I didn't mind it. I kind of liked fighting and stuff like that. It was part of my personality.

When we first started serving the LORD, my wife and I started out in some pretty lowly jobs. We were door greeters and worked in the nursery and stuff. God knew all along that He planned for me to pastor and preach, so why didn't He just start me out behind the pulpit right away? Because I would have hurt people if they had an attitude or challenged me on anything. That type of thing—offering to fight a member of the congregation—really is not good coming from the pulpit. There were some things in me that had to be sanctified and worked out.

We kept going and doing each thing, no matter how small, that God told us. Soon enough, we began to mature, prosper, and eventually stepped into our call. Just like a baby learns to hold his head up before he learns to sit up, and learns to stand before he learns to walk, there were many things I had to learn before I could take the pulpit. No one gets saved one day and steps into the fullness of their call the next. They must be shaped, molded, and trained to grow into it.

Spiritual training isn't one-sided. We don't just sit in a church on Sunday morning and receive a download of everything we need to fulfill our call for the week. God expects us to actively participate in our training and growth by following directions from the WORD, the Holy Ghost, and the pastors and teachers He has connected us to. In other words, He expects us to be faithful to train.

THE MORE YOU WALK, THE BETTER YOU'LL WALK

A modern example of this kind of faithfulness was Brother Kenneth E. Hagin whom we studied under at Rhema. He was a spiritual father to me from 1986 until he went home to be with the LORD in 2003. I'm grateful that so much of his ministry has been captured on tapes, on CDs, and in books. If you've listened to him share about his encounters with Jesus, or read his books *I Believe in Visions* and *Understanding the Anointing*, you'll remember that many times after Jesus would appear to him, He would say, "Be thou faithful and fulfill your ministry for the time is short." Jesus wasn't telling Brother Hagin to just keep working hard. No, Jesus was telling Brother Hagin, "Every time I tell you to do something, to take a step, or to make a change to do something differently, be sure to do it exactly as I instructed." This is a key, because we all want to be found faithful.

One of the things I so loved about Brother Hagin was his frankness. He often told us that for years he prayed for people with no perceived anointing on him at all. I'm sure it was true, but later in his life, there was no denying the anointing on him. For example, I remember one camp meeting in downtown Tulsa at the Civic Center. It was a big round auditorium with the platform facing the south. The auditorium was full, maybe 15,000 or so. Off to the side of the stage, there was a place for people in wheelchairs. I remember this clearly. He was preaching and suddenly stopped. He looked over at the wheelchair group, pointed, and said, "This lady..."

There were several over there and they were all saying, "Me? Me?" but he was shaking his head no.

When he finally got to the one he was pointing to, he put his hand down. He said to her, "Ma'am, when I point my finger again, the power of God is going to come on you and if you'll yield to it, then come up out of that chair and walk." So he did. And she did. But she was crippled and hadn't walked in years. When she came up out of that chair, she was quite weak and wobbly. That didn't concern him. He simply told her, "The more you walk, the better you'll walk." It was true. As she walked, she grew stronger and steadier. That was a powerful anointing, but he made sure we understood it wasn't given to him all at once. In other words, he had to stay true to the process over time.

TRAINING FAITHFULLY

I was so hungry for that kind of anointing. I told God I wanted to see those kinds of things in my ministry. Then about one o'clock one morning I was driving across the desert of New Mexico and Arizona in my pickup. Suddenly, God got in the cab of my truck and said, "You keep bugging me about more power. Son, you've got to understand, once I release it, I can't take it back. I'm leading you and guiding you and giving you tests as we go. Each time you pass, that qualifies as faithfulness. With each one, more anointing will be released into your hand. But you have to live long enough to see the full fulfillment of it."

That night, God helped me to see I could have the anointing I desired, but I had to stay alive long enough to get to that point. Take the first church my wife and I started back in July of 1988, for example. Back then, I would pray for people and not sense much of an anointing or anything. I just kept preaching the WORD and being persistent to teach. As I did, I noticed the anointing begin to get stronger over time. From this, I learned that if you are faithful to do what God says, things can be added to you[69] and you will progress. In other words, the more you walk, the better you'll walk with God.

It's the same for all of us. We have to go through some stuff—not necessarily bad stuff, but we have to get some stuff under our belts in order to walk in the fullness of the anointing He has planned for us. We have to go through some training and Romans 11:29 tells us why:

> *29 For the gifts and calling of God are without repentance. (Romans 11:29 KJV)*

> *29 For God's gifts and His call are irrevocable. [He never withdraws them when once they are given, and He*

---

[69] Matthew 6:33

does not change His mind about those to whom He gives His grace or to whom He sends His call.] (Romans 11:29 AMPC)

We see here, once God releases certain things into your life, He can never take them back. You have a free will, which means *you* can walk away from them, but God *bound* Himself to His WORD[70]. That means He *cannot* take them back[71].

Think on this for a minute. People jump and shout in services every week, "Greater anointing, LORD! Greater anointing!" Yet, have you really thought about it? If you have the full anointing of God and your soul isn't saved, what would that be like? Because if you think like the world, act like the world, and talk like the world, you might really do some damage to somebody. You might short-circuit something. Have you ever thought about what it would be like if every single word you said came to pass immediately—not just the happy prospering ones, but the negative ones too? What about the words you snap at your spouse or your kids when they get under your skin, or when someone cuts you off in traffic on the way to work in the morning? God must be able to trust you to be faithful with the anointing He gives you, because He is faithful to His WORD, and He said He won't take it back once He releases it.

This means the training time allows your soul to prosper[72] so that it won't interfere with the anointing and work against you. Each person has a different gift and call; therefore, God, being the Good Teacher, individualizes the training program for each of us. Just like we study history to learn from the successes and mistakes of others, we can study the faithful and unfaithful men and women in the Bible to understand faithfulness. It is almost a cliché in America to say, "*Many are called, but few are chosen*[73]." I wonder how many people have actually sat down and

---

[70] Numbers 23:19; Malachi 3:6; Hebrews 13:8; James 1:17

[71] Please keep in mind, I'm not saying you can never ever lose your salvation. If someone is an idiot and chooses to keep talking bad against the Holy Ghost, they can walk away if they want. Sure we know that, but we aren't interested in doing that. We've already been on the other side. We know what it is like. It is way better over here.

[72] For an in-depth study of how to prosper the soul, see my book *The Soul*.

[73] Matthew 22:14

Chapter 5: Faithfulness Requires Training

thought about the truth of that statement. Jesus was talking about faithfulness.

Faithfulness

CHAPTER 6 – FAITHFULNESS REQUIRES OBEDIENCE

CAN YOU FOLLOW DIRECTIONS?

When God tells us to do something, He usually gives pretty specific instructions. There aren't too many places in the Bible where He sends someone out and says, "Go out and do something today." Nope. Usually, He sends someone out to a specific place to do a specific job. They need to follow these specific instructions because if they don't, they might end up in a whale of trouble[74]! We see an example of this with the Hebrew children in the wilderness:

> *4 Then said the L*ORD *unto Moses, Behold, I will rain bread from heaven for you; and the people shall go out and gather a **certain rate** every day, **that I may prove them**, whether they will walk in my law, or no. (Exodus 16:4 KJV)*

That phrase *certain rate* means a specific portion. In other words, God is going to tell them a specific amount to gather. Now, why is He going to give them a specific amount? That He may prove them. What does that mean? He's going to test[75] their faithfulness by testing their ability to follow directions.

Most of you reading this book know the rest of this story. It tells us that for six days they were to gather only as much as their family could consume each day and no more. On the eve of the Sabbath, they would gather two days' worth, because there would be none on the Sabbath. The sixth day was the only day they could keep it overnight. Every other day of the week, they had to eat all they gathered[76]. These instructions were very clear and easy to understand.

---

[74] Jonah 1
[75] 11 out of 22 translations of Exodus 16:4 on http://biblehub.com/exodus/16-4.htm use the word *test* rather than prove. Ten use the word *prove*, and one uses the word *try*.
[76] Exodus 16:15-16, 19, 22-23

Faithfulness

But it is amazing how the mind can twist things. Some people thought God was just being picky. So in verse 20, we find some who didn't want to get up early and gather it in the morning. Instead, they decided they would keep some leftovers for breakfast. I can see them saying, "W00-hoo, my God supplies!" But that is not how God had it in His heart to supply them. There was a consequence—maggots. Now you'd think they would learn their lesson, but they didn't. Again, in verse 27, some of the Israelites went out on the Sabbath expecting to be able to gather manna even after Moses reminded them in verses 25 and 26 that there would be none.

At this point, if they didn't follow the instructions exactly, they missed only a day of food. But that isn't the point. If you remember verse 4, God wasn't just supplying them with food. He was trying to promote faithfulness in His people. He was trying to get them to trust Him enough to do things the way He had them in His heart, because Canaan's land was around the corner and there were giants in it. A time was coming when they would have to hear Him clearly and obey Him very carefully if they wanted to take possession of the land He was giving them.

That land was flowing with milk and honey, meaning it was their prosperous place. So when they started complaining about a lack of supply in verse 27, they were mistaken. It wasn't a lack of supply. God told them there would be none that day because He supplied it the day before. The only thing they lacked was faithful obedience and submission to authority which would eventually keep that entire generation out of the Promised Land.

Many today wonder why there is such a lack in their supply or why they never get promoted at work or at their church. Well, I can't tell you the number of times over the years that I have been driving and planning to stop at a truck stop or gas station and would hear the Spirit of God say, "Do not pull in there." Two or three times, I've had an airplane ticket in hand, and the LORD said, "Do not get on that airplane." At those times, my mind wanted to be just like those Israelites and argue about the money or the time. But I've learned to trust Him even when I'm not sure why He's telling me to do something. It has saved my money, my property, and probably even my life.

Chapter 6: Faithfulness Requires Obedience

THE ARK OF THE COVENANT

We can go all the way back through history and see that God doesn't always explain the reasons behind the instructions He gives. Exodus 25 gives us a clear example when very specific instructions were given with no explanation of why. According to the New Living Translation, the Ark of the Covenant was 45 inches long, 27 inches wide, and 27 inches high[77].

Why would God make a box that size? I absolutely have no idea. None. But we can see clearly in Exodus 25 that He gave them specific dimensions on how to make it, what to do with it, how to decorate it, how to prepare it, and then how to handle it.

> *10 And they shall make an ark of **shittim wood**: two cubits and a half shall be the length thereof, and a cubit and a half the breadth thereof, and a cubit and a half the height thereof.*
>
> *11 And thou shalt overlay it with pure gold, within and without shalt thou overlay it, and shalt make upon it a crown of gold round about.*
>
> *12 And thou shalt cast four rings of gold for it, and put them in the four corners thereof; and two rings shall be in the one side of it, and two rings in the other side of it.*
>
> *13 And thou shalt make staves of shittim wood, and overlay them with gold.*
>
> *14 And thou shalt put the staves into the rings by the sides of the ark, that the ark may be borne with them.*
>
> *15 The staves shall be in the rings of the ark: **they shall not be taken from it**. (Exodus 25:10-15 KJV)*

Many translations of verse 15 say *acacia wood* instead of *shittim wood*. Either way, that is a specific type of wood. God didn't want the ark made from just any old tree they came across. Yet, He gives no explanation as to why it needed to be from this type of wood. Also, when

---
[77] Exodus 25:10-11

Faithfulness

we get down to verse 15, we see that the staves, or carrying poles, were not to be taken out of the rings. My question is why? What does it matter if they take them out or not? What is the big deal?

The big deal is God said don't ever take them out. This is a matter of faithfulness, and it is a concept that we all deal with daily. God tells us to do something very specific and doesn't explain why. Will we do it just as He asked or not?

The writer of Hebrews tells us that "Moses was faithful to oversee the entire House of God[78]." It says he was faithful. Now that does not mean he just showed up and did it any way he wanted to do it. It meant he did it the way God had it in His heart.

God said, "Make it 45 by 27 by 27 inches. Make four rings with two on each side. Make the poles out of the same wood as you make the box. Put the poles in the rings and don't you ever take them out." It doesn't matter what the task is, and it doesn't matter if you are gifted or talented in something. Be faithful to the way He told you to do it. If He says don't ever take the poles out, then don't!

I used to be the type of person who would get hung up and say, "I wonder what would happen if I did it this way?" Thank God! He has helped get that out of me. Sometimes you can do that, and it doesn't do anything more serious than reveal what is really in your heart. But other times, if you do that, you can really mess things up. So we want to grow beyond that attitude. We want to get to a point where we can trust God enough to do everything He asks just exactly the way He has it in His heart with or without an explanation why.

When God told Moses to make the box, Moses didn't cut a board and say, "26 and ¾. Ah, that's close enough." Yet people do that all the time, then they wonder why things aren't working out for them. God took the time to be very precise and specific with Moses about how to make the Ark. In return, Moses took the time to be very precise and specific in carrying out those instructions.

This is why Moses was the leader of millions of God's people. When he was given specific instructions, he didn't settle for close enough. He

---

[78] Hebrews 3:2

Chapter 6: Faithfulness Requires Obedience

was faithful[79] and followed them exactly. As a result, God opened a new door and let him build His House, the Tabernacle[80]. Remember, to whom much is given much is required[81]. Once Moses came to know God, he was faithful with all the little things God asked him to do throughout his entire life, even when he didn't understand the reason behind the request. He was given more each time. That attitude of excellence and humble obedience is why the sea split[82] when he lifted that rod.

FAITHFULNESS TO GOD AND MEN

One Sunday, I was at home preaching. In the middle of the sermon, I just stopped and said, "I believe everybody that's here today ought to go to the grocery store and buy bottled water," then I went on preaching and never skipped a beat. Well, some of us recognized that as a Word from God. We did exactly as instructed without knowing why. Two or three days later, we found out the town had E. coli[83] in the water and, by that time, all the bottled water was gone in just a matter of a few hours. But we didn't have to worry because we already had water.

Going back to Moses, it is interesting to me that God told him to gather up some of the manna and put it in the Ark of the Covenant as a testimony to future generations that their forefathers actually ate manna[84]. Moses turned around and told Aaron to do it. Aaron took that instruction just as if God was talking because he saw that Moses had God's heart in his heart so he did it exactly as Moses told him[85]. That is the very definition of unity. Unity doesn't mean that you always agree. It means you will do it even when you don't agree. God commands a BLESSING

---

[79] Hebrews 11:23-29
[80] Exodus 25-31
[81] Luke 12:48
[82] Exodus 14:21
[83] E. coli is a bacterium that normally resides in the human gastrointestinal tract and is found in feces. However, if some strains are ingested (such as through drinking contaminated water) it can cause serious diarrheal disease (E. coli).
[84] Exodus 16:32
[85] Exodus 16:32-34

Faithfulness

where there is unity[86]. Do you realize that manna in the Ark never soured[87]? Like Aaron, we must learn to recognize when instructions from God are coming through a human vessel and honor them.

Do you remember the Old Testament prophet, Elisha? Before he was elevated to the office of prophet, he was faithful to God by faithfully serving the prophet Elijah[88]. His service to Elijah serves as a great pattern for us today. You see, I have found that as you are faithful to God, it will always create favor with men. Furthermore, if you are faithful to God, it will require being faithful to men at some point—pastors, family members, employers, etc.

Jesus is our LORD and Savior. But He no longer lives on Planet Earth. He is seated at the right hand of God[89]. When Jesus lived on Earth, He was the Great Shepherd[90], and when He left, He said, "I will not leave you orphaned and comfortless[91]. I will pray the Father to give you another comforter[92]."

Now Jesus walked in all five ministry offices when He walked on Planet Earth. But as soon as He left He said, "I'm going to instill that into men and women[93], because the Body of Christ still has to have those ministry gifts." In the local church, there is no higher office or ministry gift, than the office of the shepherd or pastor. Why? Because they live with the sheep. Many of you may not realize this, but most pastors are willing to give their life for their congregation. Your average Carl and Christy Churchmember won't do that. So, we begin to see what true gifts those that serve in these offices are to the body.

Don't get me wrong. We aren't into hero worship or anything like that, because we are all human. However, when we can see the gift of God in a man or a woman and honor it, we receive more fully from that person's

---

[86] Psalm 133
[87] Exodus 16:31-36
[88] 1 Kings 19 – 2 Kings 2
[89] Hebrews 1:3
[90] John 10:11
[91] John 14:18
[92] John 14:16
[93] Ephesians 4:8

supply. Part of honoring the gift of God in your pastors is being willing to faithfully serve alongside them and help them whenever they ask. Always keep your heart in a right attitude toward them, because God is using these human vessels to equip and supply you with everything you need for the journey ahead.

When you do this, you give God plenty to work with when He is looking to bring increase and promotion into your life. In Elisha's case, he stayed faithful to Elijah and received a double portion[94] of the anointing for ministry.

Daniel is another outstanding example for us.

> *3 Then this Daniel was preferred above the presidents and princes, because an excellent spirit was in him; and the king thought to set him over the whole realm.*
>
> *4 Then the presidents and princes sought to find occasion against Daniel concerning the kingdom; but they could find none occasion nor fault; forasmuch as he was faithful, neither was there any error or fault found in him. (Daniel 6:3-4 KJV)*

The king was considering putting Daniel in charge of the whole kingdom. The rest of the cabinet wasn't too happy about it. They were positive they could find some example of unfaithfulness to the king in Daniel. So they set spies around him to watch him, but they could find no fault or error in him because he was faithful to the king. He didn't talk bad about him, and he wasn't skimming money from the budget. He did what the king told him to do. Daniel was faithful to the king—a man.

A while back my wife wanted to do some things at our church. Someone came up to me and said, "Brother Ricky, we are always here. We are always, always here. We believe in this work. But…dah, dah, dah." They didn't agree with the changes that Sally wanted to make, even though she is the pastor of the church. They thought they were faithful because of their attendance, and that it gave them the right to disagree openly with her. Talking badly about the leadership of your church or

---

[94] 2 Kings 2:9-14

other church members is not showing love. Neither is it being faithful. Listen carefully: Faithfulness to God always involves faithfulness to people. In fact, the Bible says you cannot love God and hate people[95]. Loving God means loving people.

Let's say your pastor asks you to spruce up the landscaping in front of your church. He tells you that he wants the shrubs pulled out and replaced with a certain type of flowers and he wants the dark mulch changed to the red mulch. But you start the job and decide the red-colored mulch doesn't look as good with the new flowers as the dark mulch, so you put in the dark mulch. Did you follow the instructions given? No! It doesn't matter what you think looks better; you were given specific instructions by someone in authority.

Along the same lines, how many times has your pastor said, "Don't turn there, just listen," and you ignored him and started turning there? Maybe one time he surprised you and said, "Don't take notes, just look up," and, even though you heard him, you kept right on writing. Do you realize that is rebellion? That is the kind of stuff Jesus was talking about in Matthew 25:21, the little things.

> *21 His lord said unto him, Well done, thou good and **faithful** servant: thou hast been **faithful** over a **few things**, I will make thee ruler over many things: enter thou into the joy of thy lord. (Matthew 25:21 KJV)*

There is a reason He didn't say, "Well done faithful servant, you have been faithful in the great big things." No, He wants you to obey in the smallest, most minute, things. Because if you can obey there, then you can obey in the next step and the next.

Many times, when people are demanding explanations and trying to negotiate a different way to do an assignment, the leadership will just clam up and stop talking. They will wait for God to let them know when He has found the right person who won't argue or negotiate. They will wait for that *I have found a man* moment when God tells them who they can talk to who will carry out the plan just like they have it in their heart.

---

[95] 1 John 4:20

Chapter 6: Faithfulness Requires Obedience

If your heart is willing to go through the spiritual training and do the assignments exactly as instructed through the WORD, by the Holy Ghost, your pastor, employer, and others in authority over you, you will be found faithful because you are a man or woman after the heart of God. The longer you practice faithfulness, the more you can understand that the instructions, even if they come through a man, are actually from the heart of God. As you are found faithful to take care of even the little things, they add up to increased opportunities and promotion. But if you do not take care of them, opportunities will stop coming your way. Increased opportunities mean increased growth and increased prosperity in every area of your life.

THERE'S A PLACE FOR EVERY BELIEVER

Just like a jigsaw puzzle with a bunch of pieces, God has a plan and a place for each born-again believer. When we are each in our place and faithful to the plan, the whole beautiful picture comes together. Let me show you how I know this:

> *^{18} But now hath God set the members **every one** of them **in the body**, as it hath pleased him. (1 Corinthians 12:18 KJV)*

Because Paul stressed *every one*, that is exactly what he means. God doesn't just set people in ministry offices and leave everyone else to fend for themselves. People tell me all the time, "You know, I just can't seem to find a place where I feel like I fit." Well, according to 1 Corinthians 12:18, there is someplace they will fit. Wherever you fit, then that's where you need to be, even if it isn't in the biggest, most glamorous, church in town.

I remember I used to try to put puzzles together. I would set up the box so I could see the picture. Then I would start looking for pieces that fit on the outside edges. Usually, it wouldn't be long before I would walk away from it and leave it on the table in frustration. Sometimes in an effort to finish the thing, I would just force a piece into one of those gaps thinking, "I don't care what shape you are, you're going here!" Of course, that didn't work, even if all the pieces were used. The picture wouldn't look right, and the pieces would be all snaggle-toothed with bent ears and separating cardboard.

Some of you reading this book are like that. Your hair is all messed up, your ears are all bent, and you might even have a broken arm. You've been trying to force yourself into a place God didn't design for you. "Yeah, but I'd like to get over here in Pastor Boudreaux's church!" If you would let God put you where He wants you, you'll see it is a perfect fit.

> *28 And **God hath set some** in the church, first apostles, secondarily prophets, thirdly teachers, after that miracles, then gifts of healings, **helps**, governments, diversities of tongues. (1 Corinthians 12:28 KJV)*

Not only does God put us where He wants us, but it is also His choice as to the assignments and offices He gives us. Helps is listed here as a ministry gift. Therefore, God intends for the pastors to have help. Faithfulness means trusting God enough to do what He has in His heart when He asks you to do it. So, if He tells you to go work in the nursery, should you show up in the Youth Department? No! You should show up in the place He set up for you. The nursery? "But I don't like the nursery!" Okay, but God probably has a reason behind the request, and you should probably find out what it is by being faithful.

I remember when we went to Rhema, we walked into the building and Pastor Kenneth W. Hagin (Brother Hagin's son) started preaching a message and then said, "And if you don't like it, right back there," he was pointing toward the doors at the back of the church, "in case you can't read, E-X-I-T! Don't let the door hit you on your way out."

I started getting up. My wife said, "Where are you going?"

"I don't like this guy!" God knew exactly who I needed to help me! God told us to go to Rhema. God knew Pastor Hagin was there when He sent us there.

So often people go somewhere and say, "God sent us here," then, the pastor will preach something they don't like. They get their lips all pouty and get a little attitude saying, "Well, no man's gonna be talkin' to me like that!" God knew what would ruffle their feathers when He told them to go there, but He wants to get that out of them so He can develop them.

Chapter 6: Faithfulness Requires Obedience

Going back to that day at Rhema, Sally said, "Honey, you must have a problem, because I don't hear anything wrong." Well, now I was mad at Pastor Hagin *and* my wife. But, I stayed put, and over the years, he's loved us and helped us. We are so grateful for that ministry.

Faithfulness

CHAPTER 7 – FAITHFULNESS WITH MONEY

OBEY IN THE SMALL THINGS AND RECEIVE THE BIG THINGS

Back in 1984, when my wife and I had just come back into fellowship with the LORD, the oil industry in Oklahoma had pretty much shut down. At that time, we had four little children and just one car—an old Camaro. One day we needed to go to the store. Sally ran in while I stayed with the children in the car. An old gentleman shuffled slowly by us, and the Word of the Lord came up in me. Now I'm just sitting there minding my own business and I'm brand-new at this. But the Holy Ghost spoke up on the inside of me and told me, "Give that man five dollars."

At that time, $5 was all that we had to our name. That was it. No savings, no other money. So, I wasn't too sure about this and, looking back, I'm sure glad that man was moving slow. I needed time to discuss it with God. You know, before I got saved, I would be like, "Come on seven, Baby needs a new pair of shoes," and I'd just throw the dice. But after getting saved, I had to believe God for those shoes. All sorts of things were running through my mind: "We've got all these babies. They might need more diapers or more milk. Dah, dah, dah." I didn't know anything about anything back then. I was green!

By the time the man was about three or four cars away, I got out of my car. Mind you, I didn't have any *She Money*[96] hid. None. But I got out of my car, went over to him, and said, "Sir, I don't know if you need this or not, but it seems like I was instructed to give this to you."

"By who?" he asked.

"God."

"Thank you," he said, "You don't know how bad I need it." That was a small thing I could have easily brushed off, but I didn't.

---

[96] *She Money* is money SHE doesn't know about.

Shortly thereafter, we packed up all our belongings in a horse trailer and headed to Rhema for Bible training. We just swept out the manure, laid a blanket down, and moved. I think we had $165 to our name after we paid all our move-in expenses, and we didn't have jobs yet.

There was a special meeting at Oral Roberts University across town shortly after we arrived in Broken Arrow. The school encouraged us to go. So here we are sitting in this meeting and the LORD does it again. He specifically told us to sow $165 in the offering! I'll admit it. I clammed up and would not look at my wife. I just kept staring straight ahead hoping it would all go away. Now God won't force you to do anything, but He did keep talking to me about it.

There was something He wanted to work in us because He knew there were doors ahead of us. If I wouldn't have done the $5 at the store, then the next door wouldn't have opened, and I wouldn't have had the faith to sow the $165. So, I told my wife, "Honey, I'm getting this figure."

She looked at me and said, "You do realize that is all we have, and we've got bills to pay."

"Yes, I do."

Then she said the same thing I've heard her say so many times during our life together: "Jesus is my LORD. I trust the Holy Ghost. You're my husband and you're the head. I trust you. So whatever He's telling you, let's do it." We did it.

Not too long after, an aunt and an uncle of mine went up to Rhema and paid for the whole first year. I was so surprised, because they didn't act like very spiritual folks. Now if I wanted to ignore His leading on the seed, God would have let me work and pay that whole first year's tuition on my own. I'm sure glad I trusted Him and sowed the seed.

If you find yourself wondering why you aren't being promoted, take inventory of the things your employer asked you to do. Have you done everything He asked the way He wanted it done? What about your pastor? Your spouse? Now, what about the things God has asked you to do, big or small? Have you done them all? If your inventory reveals that you haven't been faithful to do even the little things, then you have the answer to why you aren't being given larger things.

MONEY IS A SMALL THING

Before we move on, I want to discuss a very important small thing. When we hold a dollar bill in our hand, we recognize that it is part of the natural world. But is it heaven's currency? Nope. What does it represent? The government of the United States of America. It represents gold. There is supposed to be enough gold in Fort Knox to support every dollar circulating in the economy. Most people think they need more dollars to live a BLESSED life, and sometimes they think their Promised Land is somewhere else where there are more dollars.

Let me stress something: your Promised Land is right where God placed you. We are a BLESSED church. In *How to be Rich God's Way*, Dad Dufresne tells about a time Jesus came to visit him in Peru in the mid-90s. (You can watch the entire 3-part sermon series on YouTube. I've included a link to it in the footnotes[97].) At that time, the LORD told him, "Ninety-seven percent of my people live below what I have for them" (Dufresne).

I thought about that and said, "Dear God, people are tithing and giving offerings. So what's the problem?" Faithfulness. It's not about just showing up and giving money. It is about trusting God enough to do it the way He has it in His heart. That means doing it the way you are told without giving your opinion or arguing.

Did you know that money is the very *least* thing you can be faithful with[98]. Let's consider this.

> *⁹ "And I say to you, make friends for yourselves by **unrighteous mammon**, that when you fail, they may receive you into an everlasting home. ¹⁰ **He who is faithful in** what is **least is faithful also in much;** and he who is unjust in what is least is unjust also in much. ¹¹ **Therefore if you have not been faithful in the unrighteous mammon, who will commit to your trust the true** riches? ¹² And if*

---

[97] https://www.youtube.com/watch?v=uwOEx2UWH5M
[98] Luke 11:42

> *you have not been faithful in what is another man's, who will give you what is **your own**?" (Luke 16:9-12 NKJV)*

The word *mammon* in verse 9 comes from the Greek word *mamónas* and means wealth or money (3126.Mamónas). Now, we've already established that money is natural. Money is the very least of things that one can be faithful with. It is the least thing. The prefix *super* on the word *supernatural* means above, higher, or greater. Therefore, we can understand these verses to also mean that if we cannot be faithful with natural things, then we will not be faithful with supernatural things. The inverse is also true. If you are faithful with little natural things like money, flowerbeds, and toilets, then you'll probably be just as careful and faithful with the supernatural things of God.

That's why faithfulness is so important. Verse 12 establishes that we have to be faithful with other people's stuff as well if we are to be given things of our own. That applies both naturally and supernaturally. If you can't be trusted, then that is more than likely why the things of the Spirit seem to be held up. You're not waiting on God. God is waiting on you to pass the test.

> *¹Let a man so consider us, as servants of Christ and stewards of the mysteries of God. ² Moreover **it is required in stewards**, that a man be found **faithful**. (1 Corinthians 4:1-2 KJV)*

What is a steward? Well, there are many definitions, but I like to think of it this way: one who handles the resources of another. If someone handles the resources of another, then he must be found faithful. Now faithfulness means handling the resources the way the owner wants. The resources of the church are distributed by the pastor as God leads. If I'm a steward and the pastor gives me the job to vacuum, then it is required that I handle that assignment exactly the way he said to do it. That's natural and, according to the WORD, when I finish that natural job, other things will come along.

God wants us to be faithful stewards of the resources He gives us. People think they are faithful to God, but they won't be faithful to the men and women God puts in their lives. I've learned that in order to be faithful to God, you must also be faithful to the men and women He puts in your lives.

Look at Joseph's life during his time in Egypt[99]. He was faithful to God during that time, but we also see he was faithful to the human king he served. The pharaoh trusted him. Have you ever really thought about how much land, cattle, and vineyards he bought because people were running out of food? People were selling him their entire farms just to get a little food. The king ended up with so much property he owned almost all of Egypt[100]. Joseph never mishandled other people's property. That's why he is in The Book.

THE IMPORTANCE OF THE TITHE

Now let me ask you this: who does the tithe belong to? According to the WORD, it belongs to God[101]. If we get that wrong, then we don't get the other part right either. For example, if you think, "Well, I'll tithe this week, but I have an extra bill coming up, so I won't tithe next week," then that same attitude will show up in everything else you do because tithing is the least thing that you have to get right.

We have another church in Warren, Texas. A while back, someone passed along one of our Sunday morning messages to a gentleman who does not attend our church. He later sent a message to us and said, "What you're teaching is Old Testament and we don't have to live by it."

Someone on my staff asked me, "What do you want me to do about it?"

"Nothing," I replied. "He doesn't go to church here. We don't have to do a thing about it."

This man was all ticked off when he saw a lot of money coming in. Why? Because he believes in the doctrine that you have to be poor to be spiritual. I found out a long time ago that doctrine is stupid. Where I grew up if you wanted to be real spiritual and humble, you had to be poor. But

---

[99] Genesis 39–47
[100] Genesis 47:13-26
[101] Leviticus 27:30; Malachi 3:8

that doesn't really make any sense because the things God has asked believers to do for other people and to share the gospel cost money.

His message went on to say that tithing was under the Law. Yes, that's true. But isn't it interesting that according to Genesis 14 and Hebrews 7, God incorporated tithing into the Covenant with Abraham some 400 years before the Law was ever given? So when God said, "I want you to give me ten percent of your income, your increase," I'm sure you'd agree that if I alter that, then I am unfaithful. Even if I show up at church every Sunday, Wednesday, and every special meeting, I am unfaithful if I don't tithe. That's where people get confused. They think they should get credit for just being at church.

Along the same lines, when God said, "Bring the tithe to the local church[102]," the word *tithe* literally means tenth part[103]. Therefore, you cannot tithe 6 percent. Tithe means 10 percent. I've had people tell me, "We're going to start tithing twenty percent." I told them they were wrong. The tithe is exactly 10 percent. If you want to give over the tithe, that qualifies as an offering. But that is between you and the Holy Ghost.

Faithfulness means trusting God enough to do it the way He has it in His heart. This is why we are tithers. The tithe always goes to the local church[104]. Then in the local church, there are also projects such as starting a daycare that we should be involved in. Christians should always be involved with their local church by giving offerings above the tithe. Then when there is additional money, we should sow it as God directs into other ministries.

Don't send your tithe to traveling ministers like me, or even to TV or radio ministries. Because when you get into trouble and need the help of a pastor, they won't be around to help you. Tithes and offerings keep the local church strong. When the local church is strong, we traveling ministers have a place to go. That tithe always goes to the local church because God said so. Now say out loud, "I'm faithful because I'm a tither." If money is the very least thing that we can be faithful with, then

---

[102] Malachi 3:10
[103] Deuteronomy 14:22-23
[104] Malachi 3:10

Chapter 7: Faithfulness With Money

we want to make sure we get it right, because we want greater supernatural things on us..

Faithfulness

CHAPTER 8 – FAITHFULNESS REQUIRES TESTING

TRAINING REQUIRES TESTING

Probably most of you reading this book have been to some kind of school for training and, at various points in that training, you had to take a test or two. Why? To see if you were ready for more. The trainer needed to know how well you had mastered the first part in order to see if you were ready for the next part. There may have even been a big test at the end over all the material to see if you had learned enough to be qualified in whatever you were being trained.

Similarly, when I was a kid growing up in Oklahoma, it could get mighty cold in the winter. Sometimes it would get cold enough to freeze over a pond or a creek. My little brother and I would go out and throw a rock on the ice. If it didn't sink, we'd find a bigger one and do it again. What were we doing? We were testing the ice to see if it would hold up.

Testing is a biblical principle. Paul told Timothy not to let anyone serve in even the lowliest of positions without being tested first.

> *¹⁰ But let these also **first be tested**; **then** let them serve as **deacons**, being found blameless. (1 Timothy 3:10 NKJV)*

From Acts 6, we know that deacons are servants or table waiters[105]. In today's world that is considered a pretty lowly job. But look carefully, Paul wrote that *before* they can serve as deacons they must be tested. This means they should be given other jobs within the church as a test.

Let's stop here for a moment and think about this. Who wrote this letter? Paul. Who did Paul write by or who inspired him to write this? The Holy Ghost. And who did the Holy Ghost get this from? Directly from God the Father. That's why you will find this concept all through the Scriptures.

---

[105] Acts 6:1-7

All throughout the Bible, we see the phrases *God tried* or *God tested*. But we must clearly understand God will never try or test someone with evil, calamity, sickness, or disease[106]. He put all those things on Jesus. God gives tests of obedience to see where faithfulness lies.

> *² And thou shalt remember all the way which the LORD thy God led thee these forty years in the wilderness, to humble thee, and to prove thee, to know what was in thine heart, whether thou wouldest keep his commandments, or no. (Deuteronomy 8:2 KJV)*

Let's also look at this in the New Living Translation:

> *² Remember how the LORD your God led you through the wilderness for these forty years, humbling you and testing you to prove your character, and to find out whether or not you would obey his commands. (Deuteronomy 8:2 NLT)*

As I said earlier, Abraham had to learn how to trust God and God needed to know that He could trust Abraham. The same thing applied to Noah, Moses, David, and to all of us. God wants to know whether we will be faithful or not, so He will give us tests over the course of our journey here on Planet Earth.

> *And it came to pass after these things, that God did **tempt** Abraham, and said unto him, Abraham: and he said, Behold, here I am. (Genesis 22:1 KJV)*

Sometimes the King James language can be a little confusing if we aren't real careful about it. Take that word *tempt* for instance. When most of us see that word, we think about being enticed to sin. But James 1:13, in the Contemporary English Version (CEV), tells us, *"Don't blame God when you are tempted! God cannot be tempted by evil, and he doesn't use evil to tempt others."* So we need to study Genesis 22:1 very carefully to understand what is really going on here. Let's look at it in both the New Living Translation and the Amplified Classic Edition:

---

[106] James 1:13

Chapter 8: Faithfulness Requires Testing

*Sometime later, God **tested** Abraham's faith. "Abraham!" God called.*

"Yes," he replied. "Here I am." (Genesis 22:1 NLT)

*After these events, God **tested** and **proved** Abraham and said to him, Abraham! And he said, Here I am. (Genesis 1:22 AMPC)*

So we see here, God wasn't being evil and trying to trick Abraham into sinning, He wanted to test his obedience. That is not evil. Why was God testing him then? To see what was in his heart and to see if he would be faithful. After a while, God found Abraham to be what? Faithful. This shows us *there will be tests*. We can be sure of it. Say this aloud, "I ain't flunking this one!"

In 1 Kings 15, when God told King Saul to utterly destroy the Amalekites, it was a test. But it wasn't the only test Saul ever faced. It was one of many. Abraham faced many tests, as did David and Noah and as each of us will today. This isn't an unusual concept; we even test our own children before we give them more freedom.

For example, we still have a couple of children at home. When one of them turned 16 and learned to drive, I bought her a Jeep. One of the first things I did with her was give her a test. I told her to go to the grocery store, buy a gallon of milk, and come right back. See, I know exactly how long it takes to do that. What was I testing her on? Her faithfulness to do as I said and not go cruising all around town. If she goes and comes back on time, then we'll let that sit for a time. A little later, we'll give her another test. Over the process of time, as she proves herself faithful to do what we have in our hearts, her freedom with that Jeep will increase.

THE TEST OF THINGS

Years ago, we had some friends who had just built a beautiful five or six-bedroom home. I mean, it was a beautiful house. The husband told me one time that they had no more than finished construction when the LORD began dealing with him to sell it, because He wanted them to go overseas.

Now, this couple had five little bitty kids. He told me, "I knew it was in there, but I wouldn't even acknowledge it."

Finally, he asked his wife, "Has God been talking to you about something?" She reluctantly nodded. They eventually got together and realized they both received the same message at about the same time. Their hearts were finally softened to it and they grabbed hands and went before the LORD and told Him, "LORD, we told you we would do what you said. We want you to know that we are willing. We will put the house on the market to sell it, and we'll go."

To which the LORD replied, "No. I just had to make sure that the house wasn't more important than I was. Go ahead and live in it." Now I know God knows everything, but sometimes He needs to know what is in your heart especially when it comes to things. God isn't against His kids having nice things. But quite often, He will ask us to give up some of our things to see if we have the things or if the things have us. If He asks us to give something up and we can't do it, it's a big fat warning sign we have a heart issue that needs to be addressed.

"THESE TEN TIMES"

I wonder if you have ever said, "My kids are testing my patience today!" Probably most of us have said something like that. What does it mean? For most of us, it means that someone is not listening to us or doing what we ask them to do; consequently, we find ourselves frustrated with them. Does God ever get frustrated with us? Sure He does. Let's look at Numbers 14:20-23 and see what God said to the Israelites about their tests:

> *20 Then the LORD said: "I have pardoned, according to your word; 21 but truly, as I live, all the earth shall be filled with the glory of the LORD— 22 because all these men who have seen My glory and the signs which I did in Egypt and in the wilderness, and have **put Me to the test now these ten times**, and **have not heeded My voice**, 23 they certainly shall not see the land of which I swore to their fathers, nor*

Chapter 8: Faithfulness Requires Testing

shall any of those who rejected Me see it. (Numbers 14:20-23 NKJV)

God is saying they tested His patience ten times when they did not heed His voice or do things the way He had it in His heart. What were those tests? On *The Good Book Blog*, Dr. Dave Talley, a pastor and professor at Biola University, has suggested the following ten events where the Hebrew children tested God's patience (Talley):

"These Ten Times"

Exodus 14:10-12	At the Red Sea, when Pharaoh's army was about to catch up with them, they were afraid and accused God of bringing them to the desert to die.
Exodus 15:22-24	At Marah where they found bitter water, they complained that they had nothing to drink.
Exodus 16:1-3	In the Desert of Sin, they got hungry and complained again that God had brought them there to kill them with hunger.
Exodus 16:19-20	In the Desert of Sin as they paid no attention to Moses concerning the storing of the manna until the morning
Exodus 16:27-30	In the Desert of Sin as they disregarded Moses concerning the gathering of the manna on the seventh day
Exodus 17:1-4	At Rephidim as they complained for water and were ready to stone Moses over it
Exodus 32:1-35	At Mount Sinai Aaron led the people in making the golden calf
Numbers 11:1-3	At Taberah where the people displeased the Lord with their complaining
Numbers 11:4-34	At Kibroth Hattaavah in the grumbling provoked by the rabble for meat

Faithfulness

Numbers 14:1-3 | At Kadesh in the Desert of Paran when the people refused to receive the good report of Joshua and Caleb

That is a lot of disobedience, folks. Do you understand God just wanted to get them to a point where they would come to trust Him? But after ten tests, they still didn't trust Him. You see, God wanted the nation of Israel to be such a mighty, healthy, prosperous nation that anyone who passed by them would look and say, "Look at them. God is their God."

He wants the same thing for us. Our places of worship, our marriages, our personal lives should all flourish and prosper so that everyone knows who is our God. But for that to happen, He needs something from us. What is that? Faithfulness. What is our definition of faithfulness? Trusting God enough to do it exactly the way He has it in His heart when He asks us to do it.

When God asked Abraham to leave the land of the Ur of the Chaldees, it was a huge step. God was asking him to leave everything and just about everyone he knew. Then later, when he was older, God asked him to do something very strange. Sarah got up one morning and saw him sharpening his blade. She asked him what he was doing, and he told her, "We're going to do the covenant and circumcise all the guys."

I can imagine she said something like, "You're going to do what?"

He said, "We're going to circumcise all the males. Last night God told me to do it today." You see, he had already learned, no matter what God asked him to do, he could trust God. He did whatever God told him to do. He wasn't hesitant about it. He didn't argue. He didn't complain. He just immediately obeyed and that is why he is in The Book[107].

If God tells you to go to Africa, you respond with, "Yes, Sir! When?"

If He tells you, "I want you to start a mentoring class."

"Yes, Sir! Tell me how You want it done. I'll do it."

As you walk in faithfulness, everything around you that you touch will begin to bloom. When people ask, "How do you increase so much and so consistently?"

---

[107] Genesis 17

Chapter 8: Faithfulness Requires Testing

Answer them, "To God be the glory. I trust and obey.".

Faithfulness

CHAPTER 9 – THE HEART OF FAITHFULNESS

FAITHFULNESS IN THE HARD PLACES

Before I go on, I want to be clear: We are redeemed from poverty and sickness. Glory to God! Those counterfeits come from the devil to ruin things. God never leads us into sickness or poverty. He put those things on His Son. However, there are times that the Holy Ghost will lead us places that are every bit as challenging. Redemption doesn't mean we won't get into some hard places. In the middle of it, we might be so uncomfortable we're rebuking Satan because we don't understand what God is doing. Even in those times, we can trust He always has a purpose.

I said this once in a meeting and a guy came up afterward and told me, "I'm redeemed from hard places."

"Well, good for you," I answered, "but you know, I've been in a few myself."

Even Jesus went through a few hard places. Luke 4 tells us that Jesus was full of the Holy Ghost and *led by the Spirit* when He went in that wilderness for forty days. That was a hard, dry place. Yet, the Holy Ghost didn't tell Jesus to take His tent or RV or even a canteen of water. He was going to live there. Nope. Holy Ghost just said the same thing He says to us: "I'll provide for you even there. It's a hard place, but you won't be there long. I know it is uncomfortable, but I will take care of you."

This reminds me of when I was growing up, and we would butcher animals. Every year, when it started to get chilly, we'd say it was hog-killin' time. What did we mean by that? Well, we could butcher a hog in the daytime and hang him up in a tree overnight to drain, because it was cool enough the meat wouldn't spoil. The next day, we would cut off the fat and Momma would render the lard. A lot of times when rendering the lard, the heat would cause some stuff to float up to the top and you'd have to skim that off. You know, if you haven't ever been in any hard places, there is probably a lot of stuff still inside you that needs to come up and out.

The hard places are God's refining fire[108]. He needs to get stuff out of us because some stuff can really hurt people when you are standing before them. And if you start hurting God's people, you're going to get into trouble. He doesn't want that for you or them. So don't be too anxious to get before people. For now, just be happy to work with chairs and vacuum cleaners. If you kick that vacuum when it isn't working, then you can repent and call it blessed. Over time, that junk will get out of you.

I've noticed over the years that some of the leadings took me through difficult places because there were things in me that really needed to be dealt with once and for all. When that happens, if you don't allow the Holy Ghost to lead you there, then those things won't be dealt with and they will hinder you from being promoted. If God can't yet trust you to handle things properly at your current level, then He certainly cannot trust you to handle them properly at the next level He has for you[109].

Additionally, don't forget that everyone else's call is different from yours. Maybe God is going to have you do some stuff that nobody else is doing exactly that way. They won't go through the same things that you are going through because you are unique.

THE HEART ISSUE

Sometimes, especially when I was young in the LORD, God would tell me to do certain things like run the chairs in a service. I'm serious. He would say to me, "I want you to go run those chairs," and my right leg would get to quivering.

I knew it was time to go run, but I didn't want to do it. I would argue, "LORD, I don't want to do that. It will just draw attention." Or, sometimes, I would say, "LORD, I would really like to get up and give a testimony."

---

[108] Malachi 3:3
[109] Luke 16:10

Chapter 9: The Heart of Faithfulness

He would ask me, "What about running the chairs? I asked you to do that?" because I hadn't done what He asked me to do originally. Each time I argued, the anointing would lift. Then I would leave the service and have such a problem on the way back to the house. You see, there was something that needed to be worked out of me. I thought I could get away with not doing what God asked, or by countering with something more appealing to me—something from my heart instead of His. But God had a bigger plan than my momentary discomfort.

Eventually, as I was faithful to obey Him, I got to the point where I never did want to get up in front of folks. At that point, God said it was time to start preaching. Why? Because I cooperated with His plan and He was able to get the stuff out of me that didn't belong in there. That probably would never have happened if I kept thinking I had a better idea.

Saul struggled with this too. He thought he should get full credit for being faithful just because he showed up, went to war, and did the usual and customary things people always did in a war. He didn't understand why it mattered so much to God that he takes care of every single instruction he had been given.

Wasn't it good enough to get most of it done? No, it wasn't good enough to do most of it and ignore the rest, because faithfulness is trusting God enough to do it the way He has it in his heart when He wants it done. It means completing every step in the process.

This is where many people get confused about faithfulness. They say, "I go to church."

"Yes, that's wonderful. But did you do everything else God told you to do?"

"I go to church," they repeat.

"Well, have you done what God told you to do at the church?"

"I go to church!" they insist, because they're not getting it. They don't understand there is more to this than just showing up for church services.

When people confuse faithfulness with just showing up, they can easily ignore, or refuse to do, what the pastor asks. Then when things don't work out for them, they defend themselves the same way Saul did: "Well, I go to church. I showed up. Why is this happening?"

For example, if their pastor says, "We'd like for everyone to be here about ten minutes early so we can greet our visitors and all be ready to start the service on time."

In their hearts, they retort, "Hold on there. He can't tell me what time to show up for Sunday service!" Did you catch that? It's not the issue of time. It's the heart issue coming to the surface. There is something rubbing their fur the wrong way, and it is time to deal with it. The key here is to always remember that when a pastor or anyone else in authority asks you to do something, always respond as unto the LORD[110], because He is the One to whom you are ultimately responsible[111]. Since the pastors have God's heart, their sheep should have their pastors' hearts.

But it isn't just the baby Christians who get it wrong. Saul was the anointed king, the leader of the nation, and he didn't understand either. Mature Christians and experienced church leaders can get confused on this subject too. I've had several conversations go along these lines:

Someone will tell me, "I answered the call. I am a minister."

"Have you done what God told you?"

"Well, I have answered the call."

"Have you done what God told you? Are you doing it now?"

"Well, I don't want to go overseas. I want to stay in the US."

Ministers, if God has asked you to do something, no matter how big or small, make sure you do it. You can trust Him. Don't hold back. Remember the young boy with the five smooth stones and the bold confession of faith. It took only one throw to land that giant on his back because he trusted his God would guide it.

---

[110] Colossians 3:23
[111] Hebrews 4:13

Chapter 9: The Heart of Faithfulness

NATURAL TALENT DOES NOT SUPERSEDE FAITHFULNESS

Along the same lines, pastors will often see people want to get involved in something because they are naturally gifted or talented in that area. Yet the pastors cannot trust those same people because they always think they know a better way to do it. We must always be careful not to confuse natural talent with faithfulness. It doesn't matter if you are naturally more talented or gifted in an area than the person giving you the assignment. If you didn't do what was in their heart, because you used your natural gifts and talents to do it a different way, then you were not faithful

While we are here, let me meddle just a little bit more. Have you ever been on a job where the boss tells the team to do something a specific way? Then when he leaves, somebody pipes up and says, "I know he said to do it this way, but I have a better way to do it. Let's do it this way instead. It'll be better." That isn't right. They are not being faithful to their employer. If there were clear instructions given, you need to follow them.

It is a different story if he gives liberty and says, "This is the result we need. I don't care how we get there, just figure it out." But that isn't what I'm talking about here. I'm talking about when clear and specific steps have been given, then that should be the only way it is done. Understand this, if you have trouble or difficulty with a boss or person of authority such as a pastor in your life, then you will have trouble with God. Why? Because this isn't a boss problem, a co-worker problem, a pastoral problem, or even a God problem. It is a submission problem. It is a heart issue that must be dealt with.

Remember when Samuel went to King Saul after the battle with the Amalekites[112]? In today's language, that conversation would go something like this:

"Saul, did you do everything God asked you to do?"

"Yes, Samuel."

Saul should have muzzled those sheep, because they told on him. They were probably calling out to Samuel, "Bah, we're over here, bah, behind the stalls, bah."

---

[112] 1 Samuel 15; 1 Kings 15

"Then what is that I hear?"

"Oh, that? It's nothing. Don't worry, those aren't our sheep. Those aren't our goats."

"Really, Saul? I wasn't born yesterday. Where did you bury Agag?"

"Hmm…well…see…he ain't dead quite yet. I was going to parade him through the city first and then kill him. We want to show everybody that we got him!"

No! Those are heart issues. He had a problem submitting to authority. Let God blow your horn. Don't toot your own. Let Him exalt you[113].

The same applies to us. When the pastor relates something that is in his spirit, it is not okay to take that and do it the way you think it should be done. When God asks you to do something, it is not right to take what is in God's heart and change it to what's in your heart. Like David, we must do what God wants in the way and the time that He wants it done. We need to carry out His plan fully.

IS YOUR FUR RUBBED WRONG?

Let's take a little deeper look at the heart issue. I've said it many times already: People want to think they are faithful to God simply because they show up to church. But these same folks don't do some of the very things God says in the Bible to prosper in *all* their ways. For example, they never tithe or give more than a dollar or two in the offering plate. Yet the Bible says the tithe belongs to God[114]. Or if the pastor asks them to do something, they won't do it because they reason, "He's only a man." In those cases, God has nothing to work with because, if you have faith in Him, you should trust Him and do what He says, even if that request is coming through a human vessel such as a pastor. Often, there are things coming in your future that depend upon you faithfully completing the assignments you're given today. If you don't complete today's assignment, that thing depending upon it cannot manifest.

---

[113] James 4:10
[114] Leviticus 27:30; Mark 12:17

Chapter 9: The Heart of Faithfulness

Let me share a practical example to help you see what I mean. Years ago, there was a lady at our church who always went back and forth to India on mission trips. One time, after she came home, the LORD told me to ask her to work in the nursery because He had a plan to do something for her through Sally and me.

"Give her one year in the nursery and then you help her every month for the rest of the time she's here," He said. Sally and I agreed to the plan and I asked Him if I could tell her, but He said, "Absolutely not."

So I went to her and told her, "Sister, we would like to have you work in the nursery."

Her immediate response was, "I hate kids." I just smiled.

She never did help in the nursery. There were negative consequences to that choice. Sally and I were ready to obey God, but we couldn't complete our part of the plan unless she completed her part first. There were steps she had to faithfully complete and she chose not to take them. Therefore, she couldn't fully access the provision God had planned for her[115].

She was upset all the time because she struggled to get partners to support her work in India. She couldn't understand why this happened. Even though she was mad and confused about the lack, she never bothered to find out why this happened. When something is rubbing you that wrong, be sure to seek God to find out why. Otherwise, you are probably going to miss out on something very important.

Speaking of getting rubbed the wrong way, I get so tickled when someone comes to my wife and asks her to pray for their job, because they have a co-worker who rubs their fur the wrong way. Most of the time, it is not the co-worker. Usually, it is something in them.

Let me expand on that with a story about a husband and wife with a cat. See, the wife loved the cat, but the husband only tolerated it. When the wife would pet the cat, its motor would get to going and it would just purr away. Well, one day, the wife was in the kitchen cooking and she could hear the cat complaining. It definitely was not purring. She peeked around the corner to see her husband rubbing the cat from the tail up. The cat did

---

[115] Philippians 4:19

not like it and was letting him know. The wife said, "Honey, quit rubbing that cat's fur the wrong way!"

He answered, "He can turn around any time he wants to."

When these people call complaining about their co-workers, I get tickled because that's exactly what I'm thinking, "Well, you can just turn around any time you want to." The ironic part is that those same people were praising God and thanking Him for that job when they first got it. They even came to church and gave a praise report about how God gave them a job. Then a few weeks later, here they are complaining about their co-workers and saying how much they hate their job.

If that has happened to you, here's the part you must realize: God knew those people worked there when He sent you. More than likely, there's nothing wrong with the co-worker, it is with you[116]. Quitting the job and going somewhere else isn't going to fix it. You'll just have to go around the mountain one more time[117]—meaning you'll have the same problem in a different location until you master it. We don't ever want to short circuit the process, because we want increase. We don't want to be dealing with these same issues 15 years from now. We want to be past them. Don't be like that miserable cat! Turn around and start seeking God about what needs to change in you rather than in your co-workers.

---

[116] Luke 6:41

[117] 1 Corinthians 10:10; Hebrews 3:15-17

CHAPTER 10 – A DEEPER LOOK AT FAITHFULNESS

LIVING THE GOOD LIFE

In the AMPC of Ephesians 2:10 Paul brings out that God has *prepared* a life for you—past tense—prepared ahead of time:

> *¹⁰ For we are God's [own] handiwork (His workmanship), recreated in Christ Jesus, [born anew] that we may do those good works which God **predestined (planned beforehand) for us [taking paths which He prepared ahead of time]**, that we should walk in them **[living the good life which He prearranged and made ready for us to live]**. (Ephesians 2:10 AMPC)*

This is the map for how you live the good life. We all know that we can trust God with our salvation. But we need to learn to trust Him with our life here and now. The only way that is going to happen is if we follow His plan and take the steps He tells us to take.

Sometimes we look around and wonder, "What am I doing on this path?" Don't worry about it. You don't really need to know as long as you know God led you onto it. I want to encourage you again, you can trust Him. He will never hurt you. He may ask you to give everything away, but there will be more coming if you obey. Romans 8:28 assures us that He has a purpose for everything He asks us to do. In fact, The Bible in Basic English (BBE) says that " *all things are working together for good to those who have love for God, and have been marked out by his purpose*[118]."

One of the meanings of the word *purpose* means to propose or to make your intentions known. When I proposed to my wife 36 years ago, I made

---

[118] In 1985, Dr. Dufresne preached *Marked Out by God* at Lester Sumrall's church. There is a video of highlight clips of that service on YouTube at https://www.youtube.com/watch?v=9nZAp73HO5c .

known to her my intention, my purpose. God will not tell you everything about your life, but when He does reveal something, He does it on purpose. There is a reason. It might be to get you to a greater place, or to get something out of you, or to make a connection that you will need later in life. It doesn't matter. God knows our future better than we know our past. In Ephesians 2:10, God made His intentions known to us—for us to live the good life.

It is God's responsibility through the Holy Ghost to lead us. But we have to remember that He is not obligated to tell us the *whys* or the *how comes* as to where He is leading us. We should come to a place where we can trust Him and say, "LORD, you told me to walk this path, and I'm going to walk it and enjoy it! I'm not going to whine about it. I'm not going to be a lily-liver[119] and gripe about it either!" Here's the deal: If you whine and gripe, you won't learn anything from the experience and you'll get to walk the path again.

Say this out loud, "It's an open book test. Don't flunk!"

Now, look at that last phrase of Ephesians 2:10: *"living the good life which He prearranged and made ready for us to live."* That's God's plan for you right there. He doesn't want you living in lack and poverty. He wants you living the good life. But you have to make sure you get on the right path first and be willing to walk down it with cheerfulness and rejoicing saying, "Thank you, LORD, for leading me and directing me. I know You are guiding me. I don't know what I'm doing over here other than You said for me to be over here. So I'm glad to be here!"

> *5 Trust in the* LORD *with **all thine heart**; and lean not unto thine own understanding.*
>
> *6 In **all thy ways acknowledge him**, and he shall direct thy paths. (Proverbs 3:5-6 KJV)*

Look at Proverbs 3:5-6 carefully. What does it look like? It looks like steps to me. It looks like living. It looks like your life. Qualify the phrase *all thy ways*. What exactly does that mean? Well, it means in everything. Who are we to acknowledge? God. Does He want to be involved in every

---

[119] Weak or lacking in courage; cowardly; pusillanimous (Lily-Livered).

aspect of your life? Yes. Even in your business affairs? Yes. What about your marriage? Yes. Your ministry? Yes, He should be involved.

He wants to be involved in every aspect of our lives, and what does He promise to do when He is? Direct our paths. Therefore, trusting God is about understanding He knows more than we do and allowing Him to lead us places where we did not know we were going. He has a purpose and a reason for each place He takes us. Very often, it is either to develop something in us or to get some things out of us.

God promises to direct our paths. Do you want God involved in your steps? Sure, we all do. So, how does that work? In other words, what are all the qualifiers before He will direct your path? Trusting Him, acknowledging Him, and dealing with your thoughts. Don't be always thinking with your head. Use your head, but don't go by it as your final authority. Don't lean on your own thoughts. So whatever God says, we're not going to try to reason it out or say, "I don't think that's God. I don't think I need to do that." Nope! Shut that up right then and instead say, "Yes, Sir! Thank You, Lord, we'll do that."

SETTLE IT IN YOUR HEART TO COMPLETE THE PROCESS

Sometimes God will tell us to do something, but we just don't know how to get it done. Or it may be a big project that takes a long time to complete. Does God view faithfulness differently in these situations? Let's take another look at Abraham. We know he was faithful and increased in both spiritual revelation and physical blessings. But *when* did he qualify for the increase?

> [12] And **the father of circumcision** to them who are not of the circumcision only, but **who also walk in the steps of that faith** of our father Abraham, **which he had being yet uncircumcised.** (Romans 4:12 KJV)

Many think that in order to be prosperous, or to walk in the fullness of increase, you must do *everything* God asked *before* He will qualify you as faithful and bless you. But isn't it interesting, God was pleased with Abraham once he had had simply settled some things in his heart. We see here that Abraham trusted God enough that he qualified as faithful *before* he was even circumcised in the physical because he had already committed to it in his heart. God called that *commitment* faithful. So whenever God asks you to do something, do not hesitate in your heart about it. God, through tests, will always check to see what is in your heart. Why? Because true faithfulness is a heart issue.

But there is another important concept here. Look back at that phrase, "*walk in the steps of that faith.*" We must always remember that walking in the steps of anything takes time and progression. My wife and I are right at 30 years of ministry. It's been a fun run, but I must be honest and tell you there are times when I feel like we don't know much yet. I understand what Paul meant when he wrote in 1 Corinthians 13, "When I became a man, I put away childish things. Yet, I still see as through a glass darkly[120]."

God didn't tell Abraham, then Abram, about Isaac when He asked him to leave his family in Genesis 12. At that time, Abram knew only one step to take: "Leave here and go to a land I will show you." He saw through the glass dimly. When he took that step, he qualified for the next one. With each step he took, and with each test he passed, his trust in God became stronger and stronger. Eventually, he had enough trust in God to secure his place in the Faith Hall of Fame[121]. But that did not happen overnight

It was the same for Sally and me. As we began to understand this concept of walking in the steps, and as we walked with God over these last 30 years, we began to see that no matter what He asked us to do, we could trust Him. With each assignment we've faithfully completed, He has never failed to show us His faithfulness right back.

So don't be in a great big hurry to get through the process. You've got plenty of time. Remember, if we live right, we are promised 120 years[122]. That's great news! You know why? Because if you're 60, like me, then you're only halfway! That means you have plenty of time left to do

---

[120] 1 Corinthians 13:11-12
[121] Hebrews 11
[122] Genesis 6:3

Chapter 10: A Deeper Look at Faithfulness

whatever God is asking you to do. So while you are walking out the steps to come, develop a trust in the LORD.

DON'T RUSH BUT DON'T DELAY

We've seen that once we settle things in our hearts to do them the way God wants them done, He considers that faithful. We don't want to rush the processes of God and miss any steps He's given us. But by the same token, we do not want to fall into the trap of never getting to the things He's told us to do either. Let's look at Acts 13:21-22 again:

> *[21] And afterward they desired a king: and God gave unto them Saul the son of Cis, a man of the tribe of Benjamin, by the space of **forty years**.* *[22]* ***And when he had removed him****, he raised up unto them David to be their king; to whom also he gave their testimony, and said, I have found David the son of Jesse, a man after mine own heart, which shall fulfil all my will. (Acts 13:21-22 KJV*

In Saul's case, he refused to do everything the LORD asked him to do, so the LORD removed him and closed the door on his tenure as king of Israel. We have another biblical witness of this with the Children of Israel.

When the Children of Israel were finally at the Promised Land, God told them it was time to go in and take it. He promised them that He would go with them and even told them to send in 12 spies to go see how wonderful the land was. But what did they do? They didn't trust Him! They came back and said, "There are giants in the land and we are like grasshoppers in our own sight compared to them, No way! We can't do it![123]"

So the whole camp refused to go in and fight for the land that God had already given them and promised He would help them take from the inhabitants. God was so angry with them, He wanted to kill them all. But Moses interceded for the people and He relented. But at that point, He also said He wouldn't go with them[124].

---

[123] Numbers 13:33
[124] Numbers 13-14

Faithfulness

What happened next? Well, after God told them what would happen to them for their lack of faithfulness[125], they thought about it and decided the next day they would give it a go anyway. Even though Moses warned them not to go and the consequences if they did, they rounded up their guys and went in to attack. But guess what? That door had closed. God wasn't with them, and they got whipped all the way back to Hormah[126]! It's amazing how often God wants us to do something and we don't want to do it. But as soon as we see the consequences of that decision, or the situation changes a little bit, we are suddenly ready to do the very thing we didn't want to do in the first place. We ought to be ready when God's ready.

I learned a lesson from our ancestors here. God has assigned a pretty well-defined geographical area for our ministry. Being based in Oklahoma, we are centrally located in the United States, yet we find the majority of our ministry takes place in the western half. We do go down to Peru, up to Toronto, and over to Amityville, New York. But pretty much God keeps us busy in the western half. Yet I have received invitations for the Carolinas and places like that. I asked Him about it one time. His reply, "I really don't need to tell you right now. If I were you I wouldn't go."

I answered, "Yes, Sir. Thank you," and I didn't go. Some have tried to convince me that our ministry would go well over in the Carolinas and we've been assured that if we would come, there would be big crowds. But you have to realize if God isn't going, then I'm not going. You can bet, I'm not going to make the same mistake the Israelites did. That's why they are in the Book, so we can learn from them. You may think that is the craziest thing you've ever heard. But I work for God, and I figured out He's way smarter than any of us. No amount of human reasoning about the lost or the sick will outweigh what God has said. He knows those lost and sick folk are there, and He has made provision for them. He has sent other

---

[125] Numbers 14:26-38
[126] Numbers 14:39-45

people to them. If He tells me "Don't go," then I'm not going, and you shouldn't either if He tells you not to do something[127].

He did go on to tell me, "A day will come when things will be different, but for right now, don't go." By following that instruction, I'm walking a path, and I'm being found faithful because I'm trusting Him enough to do it the way He has it in His heart when He wants it done.

Along similar lines, there is one particular project, another work, that the LORD asked Sally and me to do a while back. We are moving toward it, but haven't quite got it started yet. The delay isn't out of rebellion. We are finishing some of the other projects He told us to do. That isn't the same as refusing to go or refusing to start. However, I must warn you here not to delay too long. Even if you have settled it in your heart to do what He asks, if you wait too long to do it, that door can shut.

BE PATIENT AND ALERT

Our first year at Rhema ended in May of 1987. Along about April, something was bothering me. I was watching people dying and going to hell and I was bothered. I was impatient to know what God had planned for us and I wanted to get after it. So I started bugging Him about it.

"God, what do you want us to do? Where do you want us to go?" But He never would talk to me.

Finally, after I had frustrated myself and had run out of gas on the topic, He spoke up one day and asked me, "Do you believe that I sent you and your wife to this school?"

"Sure, I know You did."

"OK. Do you think I knew it was a two-year program when I sent you?"

"Yes, Sir, I do."

"Then I'm not going to talk to you about anything else until you finish the assignment."

---

[127] Remember, the Holy Spirit even postponed Paul's preaching in Ephesus (Acts 16:6-10).

Faithfulness

Several people reading this book are probably in that same place—bugging God about the next step. But you need to realize, if you haven't finished this one step, He is not going to give you the next one. Just finish the last one He gave you. Then, because you are intelligent and He is intelligent, He will talk to you about what is next. But make sure you let Him open the next door. Don't try to do that yourself by kicking it down. Let Him do it.

Remember Gehazi? He is one of those in the Bible who just drops off and we never hear about him again. He was the prophet Elisha's helper when the captain of the Syrian army, Naaman, came to be cured of leprosy[128]. When Naaman arrived at Elisha's house, Gehazi is the one who answered the door and told Elisha who Naaman was and why he was there. In return, the prophet told Gehazi to tell Naaman to go wash in the River Jordan. Naaman wanted to reward the prophet for helping him, but Elisha said no. Gehazi didn't agree with this and decided he deserved some kind of reward for his role in helping Naaman, so he went after Naaman and took the gifts. After that, the Bible says that he and all of his descendants took the leprosy of Naaman[129]. Everyone in his entire family would be sick for the rest of their lives.

Now listen carefully. When you are in the Ministry of Helps, very often you will begin to get glimpses and bits and pieces of the anointing on your pastor. It is called a borrowed anointing. Gehazi did not have the anointing to go tell that man to go wash on his own. That came through the office of his master. I've seen many times that someone will sense the borrowed anointing working in their life and confuse that with a call to get out and go. Make sure you stay put until God says it is time to go.

I have some friends who now live out in Los Angeles. They used to be in Arizona. What a help they were. Man, they would help. They would bless that church and bless that pastor. After a while, he got to operating like Gehazi. He would sense that anointing come on him after he would preach every now and then. At some point, he started thinking it was his

---

[128] 2 Kings 5
[129] 2 Kings 5:27

Chapter 10: A Deeper Look at Faithfulness

own anointing. Eventually, he and his wife left the church and separated. He isn't even in the ministry.

Don't let the devil hoodwink you. You're smarter than that. Just keep patiently doing what God told you to do until you complete the assignment and He tells you to do something different.

BE READY TO COURSE CORRECT

Remember, the Bible tells us that if any man adds to or takes away from the WORD, then his name will be blotted out of the Lamb's Book of Life[130]. God takes His instructions seriously whether we do or not. Now God understands that there are times when we don't understand something in the WORD, and He allows us to move forward with all the light we have on the subject until we have more. But once we have more, He expects us to course correct.

For example, for years Brother Hagin preached that speaking in tongues was of the devil until he got a revelation about it and understood it. At that point, he corrected his course and began teaching it was of God. The most dangerous thing in the world is to come into the Light and then back out of it. So if you have Light on something, and you know exactly what God told you to do, then from that day forward you are responsible to do it that way.

To be found faithful, we must be careful about everything God asks us to do. We should never add to it or take anything away from it. Romans 14:23 tells us that "whatsoever is not of faith is not of God." For example, if God asks me to give Pastor Jay $50, and I reach into my pocket and get $30 instead, then I will not be able to attach the God-kind of faith[131] to that $30. I can attach the natural laws of sowing and reaping, but I cannot attach the God-kind of faith because I did not obey the God-kind of WORD.

---

[130] Deuteronomy 4:2; Revelation 22:19
[131] Mark 11:22

Faithfulness brings the increase and the promotion. That's why it is so important to be faithful in the little things[132]. Over time, my wife, Sally, and I have noted that everything we put our hand to has prospered and increased. We have truly been living the good life. Faithfulness is the key to this. Many are hungry for prosperity, but they aren't willing to do what is necessary to be faithful, or, they won't do it the way God has it in His heart.

There is something most people don't realize, Brother Hagin was in his mid-sixties when his ministry really got to cranking. That's when the anointing increased so much that the ministry went international. I was thinking about that one day and decided to ask God about it. His response was, "I got him to a place." Do you understand? Brother Hagin was diligent and a man who would do whatever God asked him his whole life. But age tempers things and brings wisdom.

What do I mean by that? Well, a lot of us, when we were younger, could care less if we owned a house or if we had a new car. In my case, I was all about racing, so I always had a brand-new Camaro. I am redeemed from slo0000000w! Amen! I may have been renting a house, but Buddy, I could outrun you in the streets! I could do a quarter-mile in less than seven seconds. I mean zoom! One time, I had a car so fast it would burn the tires off. I mean, I might not be able to go out to eat because I was burning up all that gas, but I sure could outrun you! I'm older now. I still love fast cars, but my priorities have changed. I'm sure you can relate to that. As we age, we begin to settle down and we start to see that some things just really don't matter.

---

[132] Matthew 25:21

CHAPTER 11 – FAITHFULNESS AND THE BLESSING

THE BLESSING OF GOD

When God wanted to deliver Israel from their oppressors, He found Gideon to be faithful and placed an open door before him. Though God allowed Gideon to use a fleece to understand His intentions, the open door was for promotion and increase. In other words, God was getting ready to bless Gideon and Israel in a mighty way as soon as Gideon walked through the door.

I've mentioned the BLESSING of God several times already. Now I'd like to take some time and study it out carefully. We want to be balanced in our understanding with no gaps. The BLESSING, like faithfulness, is a subject that can easily confuse people. In fact, God had to straighten me out about it, because I used to sing the song *Abraham's Blessings are Mine* by Garlon Pemberton. It goes:

> *Abraham's blessings are mine*
>
> *Abraham's blessings are mine*
> *Mine in the city*
> *And mine in the field*
> *Abraham's blessings are mine*

I would sing this song and then I would say, "I desire Abraham's blessing."

But God corrected me and said, "No, you don't. That's not scriptural." Now I have to be honest and tell you, at that time, I was a bit confused by this statement. So I asked Him to help me understand what He meant.

He said, "You want the same BLESSING that I *promised* to Abraham. But it is *my* BLESSING. It is an ability and a power that will come upon you to *produce* wealth. The wealth itself is simply a manifestation of the power. But my BLESSING does not stand alone. It stands in the midst of faith and being faithful." In other words, you gain access to it with your faith and faithfulness.

To understand the BLESSING, let's first take a look at what the Letter to the Galatians says about it:

> *13 Christ hath redeemed us from **the curse of the law**, being made a curse for us: for it is written, **Cursed is every one that hangeth on a tree**:*
>
> *14 That **the blessing of Abraham might come on the Gentiles** through Jesus Christ; that we might receive the promise of the Spirit through faith. (Galatians 3:13-14 KJV)*

For clarity, let's also look at this in the New Living Translation:

> *13 But Christ has rescued us from **the curse pronounced by the law**. When he was hung on the cross, he took upon himself the curse for our wrongdoing. For it is written in the Scriptures, "**Cursed is everyone who is hung on a tree**." 14 Through Christ Jesus, **God has blessed the Gentiles with the same blessing he promised to Abraham**, so that we who are believers might receive the promised Holy Spirit through faith. (Galatians 3:13-14 NLT)*

The NLT more clearly shows us *God* redeemed us from the curse, so now *God* can bless the Gentiles also *"with the same blessing **He promised to Abraham**."* What does that mean? It is not Abraham's. It's God's. We don't want Abraham's blessing. We want God's[133]!

> *9 So then they which be of **faith** are **blessed** with **faithful Abraham**. (Galatians 3:9, KJV, emphasis mine)*

In this verse, we see both faith and the BLESSING. But notice, both are tied to faithfulness. So, they which be of what? *Faith.* Are what? *Endowed with the power to create wealth.* With who? *Faithful Abraham.*

---

[133] In case you ever wondered, that is why we always capitalize the BLESSING in our books. We want to emphasize that the BLESSING which comes with power belongs to God, not man.

Chapter 11: Faithfulness and the Blessing

Why was Abraham blessed? *Because he was faithful.* What is faithfulness? *Trusting God and doing it the way He has it in His heart when He wants it done.*

God wants to bless us, prosper us, and promote us but we must understand His BLESSING works through faith and faithfulness. Without those, we cannot access the good things He has planned for us.

> *¹Now the* LORD *had said unto Abram, Get thee out of thy country, and from thy kindred, and from thy father's house, unto a land that I will shew thee:*
>
> **² And I will make of thee a great nation, and I will bless thee, and make thy name great; and thou shalt be a blessing:**
>
> *³ And I will bless them that bless thee, and curse him that curseth thee: and in thee shall all families of the earth be blessed. (Genesis 12:1-3 KJV)*

I want to point out that if Abram would not have left Ur, he would not have received Isaac and he would not have been in the Book. But he did leave, and God promised to make his name great. When you study that out, God was talking about increasing Abram's realm of influence beyond just his kinfolk and household servants. That applies to us today as well. As God works with us, and as we train ourselves to trust Him, we prove faithful not to abuse our realm of influence for our own personal benefit. At that point, He will grant us a greater voice or realm of influence as well —that is, making your name great.

Ultimately, God wants us to be a blessing to those around us. He wants the results of the BLESSING on our lives to overflow all around us. He wants us to be so joyful that we lift others up with our cheerful smiles, our joyful laughter, our encouraging words, and our loving actions. He wants us to be so financially stable that we can help those in need and give towards the work of the kingdom. He wants us to be so healthy that we live the full number of our days in vigor like Moses, Joshua, and Caleb. As this world gets darker and darker, God wants us to bless it with a brighter and brighter light coming from our lives[134].

THE BLESSING IS MORE THAN JUST MONEY

God told me one day, "I want to make you rich." Never misunderstand about true prosperity. Proverbs 28:20 tells us that a faithful man will *abound*[135]. Now that doesn't say increase. What does that mean? Well, John 10:10 in the Amplified tells us that the life we are supposed to have is to the full until it overflows. That is the abounding part. That's more than enough.

I shared earlier that when I was younger, I was the town drunk. Thank God that all changed when we got into fellowship with God, because that life was not abounding or rich in any sense of the word. But you know what? Through our years of serving, my wife and I have connected that if we do whatever God asks us to do, exactly the way He asked and in His timing, then it always brings us increase. It has brought a richness to our lives that cannot be duplicated by other means.

Most Christians never realize the connection between faithfulness and financial prosperity. In their limited view, they think that sowing and reaping is all there is to it. But it is not. I'll say it again: it is not. You can work your fingers to the bone and all you'll get is bony fingers.

God's BLESSING is a power. It is an endowment[136] God has promised to put on those who walk in faith and are faithful. It gives the ability to produce wealth. When we talk about wealth, I want you to remember that true prosperity (wealth) is not limited just to money. It encompasses everything good, and perfect, and helpful in this life. It is an overflowing abundance in every area of life. Let's take a look at Deuteronomy 8:18. We want to study this carefully so we can stay well balanced in spiritual matters:

---

[134] Matthew 5:14-16

[135] Abound: to occur or exist in great quantities or numbers; to be rich or well supplied in something; to be filled with or to teem with something (abound)

[136] Endowment: the act of furnishing something freely, such as financial grant for support or maintenance, or naturally, such as a sense of humor (endow).

Chapter 11: Faithfulness and the Blessing

*¹⁸ "And you shall remember the LORD your God, for it is He who gives you **power** to get wealth, that He may establish His covenant which He swore to your fathers, as it is this day. (Deuteronomy 8:18 NKJV)*

That word *power* is the Hebrew word *koach* and, in the masculine form (3581.koach), refers to the explosive dunamis power of God, or God's ability to do mighty and miraculous things through the believer (1411.dunamis). Today, many are just after the increase in finances. They never go after faith or faithfulness which is how you access the BLESSING. Or we see the opposite—people going after Jesus and nothing else. They never access the BLESSING for anything other than things they deem to be spiritual. But when we look carefully, we see that God didn't limit the BLESSING to only spiritual blessings or only physical blessings.

It means an increase in your health, in your marriage, and in else everything you do. Don't make the mistake of thinking that just because someone has a big house or a nice car they are prosperous. Before deciding, look at their health, their marriage, their work ethics, and the other aspects of their lives. From that, you can begin to see if they are truly prospering according to God's definition.

Here's an example of prosperity in my own life. Most people wouldn't recognize this as prospering, but when you see things the way God does, you can clearly understand why I say this. I've already mentioned that my wife and I had a bunch of kids. Now when you have a bunch of kids, you may forget some things that happened to each individual child because of the sheer number of things that happen over a lifetime of raising them. But I will never forget the day in Silsbee, Texas when we found Levi floating facedown in the pool. He was all swollen and black and the doctors told us that we really shouldn't bring him back because he would end up being a vegetable. But you know what? God is faithful and now Levi can preach faster than me! Glory to God! That was an increase in his health and a manifestation of the BLESSING in our lives. Our son's life was worth more than any amount of money God could have given us at that moment. God prospered our family that day when He gave Levi back to us.

THE BLESSING MAKES YOU RICH

Brother Hagin shared one time that the LORD told him, "My desire is to make you rich. If you will do what I tell you to do, then I will make you rich. I am not opposed to my kids being rich. I am opposed to them being covetous" (Pearson 20). In Mark 10, the story of the rich young ruler reinforces the principle that if you follow God, He will make you rich. Now I know you can go out and get rich by other means. It is clear in the Bible that unsaved and ungodly folks can be rich too[137]. The rich young ruler said he was good, but he went away unhappy. Later on, Jesus explained that he could have had 100 times what he gave up, if he had done what he was told and followed Him[138].

There was a day when I was just like that guy. When I first met my wife, I told her that I would be a millionaire by a certain age, and I didn't care how I got it. Well, after we got into fellowship with God, I realized something very important. I'm not *filthy* rich. I'm *righteous* rich! I'm going the way of God. It might take longer, but when I get there, I can stay where I am and keep what I've got, because the WORD promises, *"The BLESSING of the LORD makes one rich and He adds no sorrow to it"* (Proverbs 10:22 NASB). It's the same for you.

Here's another example of the BLESSING in our lives. In 1997, we drove by a big old colonial-style home on a little hill in Pawnee, and my wife said, "That's my house." Well, I just about ran my car off the road because the price tag was several hundred thousand. I just didn't have that level of faith yet. But she had it in her heart that it was hers. So I didn't oppose it. I just didn't say anything.

Over time, God began giving us steps: "Ricky, go do this meeting, Sally, do this, Ricky, travel more this year, I want you both to do this, I want you to connect with these folks, etc." Each time He told us to do something, we were quick to obey. As a result, we just kept seeing increase, and increase, and more increase. The point is, we did not bring the increase to ourselves and it didn't happen overnight. God brought it

---

[137] Mark 10:17-31
[138] Mark 10:29-30

little by little as we grew in faithfulness[139]. Paul talked about this same thing in 1 Corinthians 3:6 when he said, *"I have planted, Apollos watered, but God gave the increase."* We always need to remember this.

So we were going along at a pretty good pace. Fifteen years later, I was headed out to preach in Lockhart, Texas, which is down by Austin, and the Spirit of God prompted me. He said, "Call that guy about Sally's house today."

I didn't question. I didn't argue. I didn't push it off and get to it later in the week, because I'm at a point now where I just trust Him. So I said, "Yes, Sir." I just did exactly what He told me to do when He told me to do it. I called the guy.

He was a little surprised to hear from me and asked what I was doing. I told him I was calling to check on the house. He answered, "Well, Man, you caught me at a good time!" Now you and I both know *I* didn't. *God* knew what was going on, and He knew this was a good time to call. If I had waited until the next day, it might not have been as good. Turns out, he was building a store and he had just spent about $750,000, so he had mostly depleted his cash.

"Well, you want to sell the house?"

"Yeah, you know I want to sell the house."

I said, "Well, what is the price tag today?" He dropped $200+ thousand right then and there. We are now down to about $168,000. I told him, I believe I'll take it!

"OK. How do you want to pay for it?"

"I don't want to put any money down, and I want you to carry it for ten years," I replied.

"Sounds good to me." We moved in the next week. Amen! Glory to God!

Now that was a manifestation of the BLESSING, but the BLESSING will not produce without faith and faithfulness. Generally, it takes time for the BLESSING to manifest the increase and promotion. People quit too soon. In our case, it took 15 years to get that house. If we had quit at year 5, or even year 10, we would have missed out on the BLESSING of the

---

[139] Exodus 23:29-30; Deuteronomy 7:22

house. By the same token, if we had jumped out ahead of God, we could have put ourselves in a financial bind and ended up working just to pay for the house instead of serving God with all our hearts. You see, many know they are BLESSED because the Scripture says so. But they are so focused on the BLESSING, the power of God to produce, they forget about faithfulness. It is a very key ingredient because, without it, you won't be able to stand firm long enough to receive the benefits God has planned for you.

CHAPTER 12 – INCREASE FOLLOWS FAITHFULNESS

BENEFITS FOLLOW FAITHFULNESS

There are definitely benefits to serving God with all your heart. Look at David. He received the king's daughter as a wife, no more taxes, and a financial reward for killing the giant who was slandering God's people, Israel[140]. Those were just the immediate benefits. When you study his life, you'll see many other benefits came as a result of this event—such as favor with his countrymen and even a new job with King Saul. I want to point out, however, that those benefits include more than a mere increase in finances. They crossed the whole spectrum of David's life.

Let's look at David and his brother, Eliab, again. We know that Eliab's heart wasn't right towards God. He was disgruntled and accused David of naughtiness in his heart[141]. Basically, he was accusing David of being nosey and money hungry. But when we look at David's words and actions, we see a different story: He was not driven to action by the benefits, though he was interested in them. He was driven to action by his love for God and Israel.

> *David asked the men standing near him, "What will be done for the man who kills this Philistine and **removes this disgrace from Israel? Who is this uncircumcised Philistine that he should defy the armies of the living God**?" (1 Samuel 17:26 NLT)*

> *David said to the Philistine, "You come against me with sword and spear and javelin, **but I come against you in the***

---

[140] 1 Samuel 17:25
[141] 1 Samuel 17:28

name of the LORD Almighty, the God of the armies of Israel, whom you have defied. *(1 Samuel 17:45 NLT)*

David was driven to action by his love of God and country. The benefits and increase followed because God and David's country both saw he was faithful to complete that bold assignment. God honored David because David honored and trusted God in his heart.

When I teach this, some say that I'm serving God only to get things. No, I serve God because I love Him. And because I love Him, I'm going after Him with all my heart, all my soul, and all my mind[142]. I'm not money hungry. I'm hungry for the things of God. All this stuff just keeps chasing me down[143]. When I'm faithful, God can't help but pour out blessings, because He said in His WORD that He rewards those who diligently seek Him[144]. Even in the Old Covenant, in Psalm 103:2, it says, "*Bless the* L*ORD, oh my soul, and forget not His benefits.*" There are benefits to serving God! Psalm 103 provides a whole list of them.

Think about it this way: If you truly needed a job and God gave you one, you'd be really grateful. You'd be thrilled about it and see it as a way to gather your tithe for the local church and seed for sowing. Of course, you'd go in and work hard for your employers. After a while, they might come to you and say, "You've been a good employee. You have worked hard. You've shown up and been faithful to be on time. When we asked you to stay a few times, you were willing. So now we'd like to give you benefits."

How many people in their right mind would turn that down? How many people would say, "Insurance? 401K where you match my half? Nah…I'm just happy to be here." Like I said, they wouldn't be in their right mind if they did.

Yet there are Christians like that with God. They say, "I'm just so thrilled to be saved," and they act like God doesn't have any other benefits. Isn't it amazing? Say this out loud, "*Bless the* L*ORD, O my soul: and all that is within me, bless his holy name. Bless the* L*ORD, O my soul,*

---

[142] Luke 10:27
[143] Matthew 6:33
[144] Hebrews 11:6

and forget not all his benefits[145]*!* There are benefits to faithfully serving God! And God wants me to receive them!"

FAITHFULNESS TO GOD BRINGS INCREASE

A faithful man shall abound. I am not interested in just getting along. I'm after abundance and overflow in every area of my life and ministry.

> *[20] A faithful man **will abound with blessings**,*
> *But **he who hastens to be rich will not go unpunished**.*
> *(Proverbs 28:20 NKJV)*

Does that Scripture say that a faithful man will live on *Just Barely Get Along Street*? No! It says a faithful man will abound with blessings. However, we must pay close attention to the last part, *but he who hastens to be rich will not go unpunished*. We need to understand that we are not out to be rich for the sake of riches. We are out to be BLESSED and by being BLESSED we are going to be rich. Remember, God told Abraham, "In blessing I will bless you. I will make your name great. You are going to be a great blessing[146]." Then the Bible also tells us how Abraham was rich in silver, gold, and cattle[147]. So a faithful man shall abound in blessings.

Most people believe God *for* favor. Yet if you truly study it out, those who *walk in faithfulness* find favor walks with them[148]. That's why it always seems like those who are faithful are always being promoted because favor comes with faithfulness. I'm out to walk in every level God has for me. How about you?

Now let's look at what Jesus said about faithfulness in Matthew:

---

[145] Psalm 103:1-2
[146] Genesis 17:2; 22:17; Hebrews 6:14
[147] Genesis 13:2
[148] We have a mutual friend, Sister Kate McVeigh, who has written two books on favor—*The Blessing of Favor* and *The Favor Factor*. These are wonderful books. I highly recommend them for further study. She has them available for purchase on her website. http://www.katemcveigh.org

> *21 His lord said unto him, Well done, thou good and **faithful** servant: thou hast been **faithful** over a **few things**, I will make thee **ruler over many things**: enter thou into the joy of thy lord. (Matthew 25:21 KJV)*

Let me ask you this: What brought the increase? Faithfulness! It is important to understand that just as faithfulness is more than just diligence or hard work, increase or prosperity is more than just sowing and reaping. Sowing and reaping is a law. And, like most laws, there are rules to follow within it. For example, Proverbs 10:5 talks about a young man who slept during the time of harvest. This tells us there are rules for reaping. Faithfulness is one of those rules—doing what God says *when* He says to do it. You may be faithful to sow the seed, but if you sleep through the harvest, there will be no increase in finances from the sale of that crop.

Furthermore, Peter wrote that if we are faithful and humble to do what God asks, when He asks, and in the way He asks, He will exalt us[149]. This means every time a person is found faithful, God will promote them and give the increase. Don't ever worry about being behind the scenes. Just keep doing what God says and let Him worry about everything else. If He wants you to be on TV or the radio one day, He'll get you on there. Don't worry about it. Just keep doing what He says when He says to do it. If He told you to go to small churches throughout the world, then that's what you do. He'll take care of the rest. If He told you to work in the nursery, then do that. You just keep showing up and doing what God told you to do. He'll see to it that a greater door of increase will open to you as He finds you faithful.

THE ANOINTING IS TIED TO FAITHFULNESS

Let's take a quick look at two promotions in the Bible. We can learn a lot about faithfulness and the anointing through each of these men's promotions.

---

[149] 1 Peter 5:6

Chapter 12: Increase Follows Faithfulness

*¹⁵ And the LORD said unto **him**, Go, return on thy way to the wilderness of Damascus: and when thou comest, **anoint Hazael to be king over Syria:***

*¹⁶ And Jehu the son of Nimshi shalt thou anoint to be king over Israel: and **Elisha the son of Shaphat of Abelmeholah shalt thou anoint to be prophet in thy room.** (1 Kings 19:15-16 KJV)*

God is speaking to the prophet Elijah in these verses. Now, who told Elijah to *anoint Hazael to be king over Syria*? God did. Then, at the end of verse 16, God tells him to go and *anoint Elisha to be a prophet*. Where? In Elijah's room. In other words, Elisha is going to train under Elijah. Who told Elijah to do that? God. Every time a person is found faithful, God will open doors. It has nothing to do with leadings, but everything to do with faithfulness. In this case, these two men, Hazael and Elisha, had been found faithful and now God was opening doors of promotion and increase for each of them. Keep in mind, during the Old Covenant, the anointing of the Holy Spirit came upon prophets and kings to help them fulfill their duties. So when Elijah anointed these men in the natural, they also received an increase spiritually.

A lot of folks want the anointing, but they aren't faithful with the $5 they have in their wallet. You have to get the money right before you can get the anointing to raise the dead. A lot of people don't have enough anointing on them to heal a fly. They wonder why things don't work for them, yet they don't examine their lives to see if they missed any steps God told them to take or any assignments He told them to complete[150].

*² Now the most important thing about a servant is that he does **just what his master tells him to**. (1 Corinthians 4:2 TLB)*

Just because we're not faithful with $5 in the beginning, doesn't mean we can't get to the place where we can be. We're on a journey. God is leading us places and taking us through some things so He can get that

---

[150] Romans 4:12

Faithfulness

junk off of us. We want to get to the place where He can trust us with more than what we have on us now.

As God begins to work with us, He will talk to us about the things He wants us to do. But sometimes, especially when we are young in the LORD, we don't always hear so clearly. You may know that you should help, but you don't know quite where. That is when you go to the pastor and talk to him. He'll have plenty of ideas where you can put your hand to the plow[151] and faithfully serve.

Brother Hagin openly shared with the Rhema students about how he would often pray for the sick when there was no healing anointing. By sharing this with us, we came to understand it is a process. He had to go through the same training and testing process as everyone else to prove himself faithful over time to handle increased anointing. Most of us only saw him at the tail-end of his life and ministry when there was a tangible anointing. We saw people coming off stretchers and out of wheelchairs. When that is all you see, it is easy to think that he had always operated at that level. He did not.

I remember being in a meeting with him in 1996[152]. We broke 35 chairs that night. I believe that was a record. We had a ball in that Holy Ghost meeting. It was so fun because we were just flowing and laughing and dancing. He walked around that sanctuary and would lay hands on the person at the end of the row and the whole row would fall under the power of the Holy Ghost. At one point, he just pointed to a section and the whole section fell under the anointing. Towards the end of that meeting, he shared that not getting to the Holy Ghost meetings soon enough after the LORD told him to do them caused him to have an irregular heartbeat and high blood sugar after 61 years of divine health. As he was telling this, he said the LORD told him, "When you obey Me, a stronger anointing will come on you. When that anointing is in full manifestation, people who get within three feet of you will start laughing. When they get within three

---

[151] Luke 9:62
[152] This event occurred February 22, 1996, at Winter Bible Seminar. Here is a link to the entire sermon video:
https://www.youtube.com/watch?v=AbNqrdTUD70

Chapter 12: Increase Follows Faithfulness

feet of you, they will fall under the power. Not all of them. But with that strong anointing, thirty percent of them will. It will be increased." (K. E. Hagin)

I saw that increased anointing working in his life. In some meetings, he would have to get within two or three feet. In others, he would just get in the vicinity of people and they would go wild. I'm interested in that kind of increase. We're not going after money. But you have to understand, if we keep going after God like that, then everything is going to increase. God said if we focus on Him first, then He'll add everything else to us[153].

---

[153] Matthew 6:33

Faithfulness

Part Two – Open Doors and Ministry Rooms

CHAPTER 13 – THE OPEN DOOR BEFORE YOU

Remember that game show from the 70s, "Let's Make a Deal" with Monty Hall. It has made a comeback with Wayne Brady. It is famous for having doors and curtains, and members of the studio audience are picked at random, usually the ones dressed in the craziest costumes. They are then offered something of small value by the host and given a choice to keep it or exchange it for a different item. The problem is, the different items were always hidden behind a curtain or in a box and the person had to pick between the curtain or box or cash. They didn't know if they were going to pick something better or something worse. Sometimes, they won big new cars and stuff. But sometimes, they got *zonked* and won a rattletrap car, a purse made of bacon, or something else equally silly (Let's Make a Deal).

While that game show may be very entertaining, I'm sure glad real life isn't that way. God doesn't work that way with our opportunities for increase and promotion. We don't have to dress up and act all crazy to get His attention. We don't have to guess which doors to walk through for the promotion and increase, because He'll tell us. Furthermore, we should not be looking around at someone else's door either. We just have to trust Him and do what He has in His heart when He wants it done.

THE INCREASE ON THE OTHER SIDE

Let's look at what Paul said about open doors in his letter to the church at Corinth:

> *⁹ For a **great door and effectual**[154] **is opened unto me**, and there are many adversaries. (1 Corinthians 16:9 KJV, footnote mine)*

---

[154] Effectual: producing or capable of producing an intended effect, results, outcome, or influence (Effect)

Since we know believers are to be led by the Spirit who lives on the inside of them, the inward Witness, we understand this verse is not referring to guidance or direction. Therefore, the great door in 1 Corinthians 16:9 is open for opportunity, for increase, or for promotion because someone has been found faithful[155].

Over the years, my wife and I have noticed increase has followed each time we walked through a door God opened for us. Always. Yes, there were increased finances, but it was more than just money and properties. Just like Gideon, there was greater anointing. There was a much greater insight into the Scriptures. It's amazing! Scriptures we've read before suddenly jump out at one of us and we'll say, "I've never seen that before!" Amen! Thank God for what we have seen, but there's a lot in there we haven't seen yet.

We also noticed there is usually quite a gap of time between each door that God opens for promotion and increase. This is because each new door requires a greater degree of trust in God on our part, along with greater faith and faithfulness. Additionally, each new door requires deeper heart issues to be dug up and dealt with. Things that weren't a problem before may now suddenly come to the surface.

Let's look at what Jesus said to the church at Philadelphia about spiritual doors:

> *7 And to the angel of the church in Philadelphia write; These things saith he that is holy, he that is true, he that hath the key of David,* **he that openeth, and no man shutteth; and shutteth, and no man openeth;**
>
> *8 I know thy works: behold, I have set before thee* **an open door, and no man can shut it***: for thou hast a little strength, and hast kept my word, and hast not denied my name. (Revelation 3:7-8 KJV)*

In my King James Bible, everything in Revelation 3:7-8 is in red. That means Jesus is speaking and John is recording it. According to this Scripture, if God opens any door, can any man shut it? No. They might not

---

[155] Revelation 3:8

like the promotion you are going into, but God says no man can shut it. Now think carefully here. If no man can shut it, can *any* man open it? No. Only the one it is intended for can open it through faithfulness. So if faithfulness opens the door, what shuts it? Unfaithfulness. By the same token, if God shuts a door, don't stand there kicking it and trying to force it open.

Remember, we are not talking about the door of salvation, but doors of increase and promotion. Jesus told us that He's going to open some doors and He will shut some. I think we can all agree that open doors are always good. Think about it. If you get up from your chair right now and head out your front door, if it's shut and you don't open it, you're going to bang into that puppy. If you keep trying to walk through that closed door, you'll probably end up with a knot on your head big enough for a calf to suck! You can butt up against it all you want, but it sure is easier to go through it when it is open. The same principle applies in the spirit realm. Let's go through a door God has opened. It'll be way easier.

FAITHFULNESS IS THE KEY

Take a look at this excerpt from Brother Hagin's book, *Jesus the Open Door*:

> *"Jesus has opened the door of provision and blessing to us. As we attend to the Word and walk in close fellowship with Him, He also continues to open other doors for growth, opportunity, and service in our lives.*
>
> *Jesus opens wonderful doors of service for us! When we are obedient to walk through the doors of service the LordD opens to us, we will be amazed at the rich spiritual growth that will take place in our own personal lives. God abundantly rewards those who are obedient to His will.*
>
> *However, it is amazing to me how many believers want to do something for God, yet they are waiting until they can do something **big** for Him. But, if they won't do something **little** for God, they won't ever do anything big for God.*

Faithfulness

That's why it is so important to start out serving God wherever you are. Whatever small door He opens for you, walk through it, so He can open bigger doors of service for you. (K. E. Hagin, Jesus the Open Door *82-83)*

It amazes me as well how God will pick someone out of a crowd and give them an assignment, and then people will begin to wonder, "Well, how come they get to do that?" Simple, it was God's choosing. But it wasn't on God's side only. The man or the woman He chose had a lot to do with it because they were willing to do what He asked. Faithfulness is the key to opening that door.

It is exhausting to deal with someone who wants to argue or complain about everything. I'm not saying God gets tired, but I am saying it is a whole lot better when a person is willing to do whatever He asks without arguing, complaining, or debating.

Most of us have either been a kid or have kids. So let me use kids to illustrate what I mean. My wife and I have a wealth of kids. In other words, we have a lot. Some are ours, some are adopted, and some just lived with us and we claim them as ours. We never let them try to negotiate with us about church. It didn't matter how late they were out on a Saturday night, church the next morning was non-negotiable. We never let our kids ask, "Why?" either. We just had too many of them to let them do that. Sally and I weren't about to sit around all day and explain over and over again why they had to do something. So when they asked, we just said, "Because I told you to do it. Now if you don't want to do it, let me whip on you a little bit and then you'll do it. So you go on and do your crying, and when I get back, I expect that to be done."

Let's look at a spiritual example. Pastor John could be having his quiet time with the LORD, when the LORD says, "You know, Brother Jimmy has been faithful. He has been helping and he's been doing everything I ask to take care of you. He picks up your car and washes it and he does these several other things for Me. I want you to bring him up in the Helps Ministry concerning this certain area." That wasn't Pastor John's idea; it was God's. Faithfulness will always bring you up before God[156].

---

[156] Acts 10:4 , 31

Chapter 13: The Open Door Before You

But sometimes people want to think the pastor just has favorites. No, that's not it. We operate just like everyone else—by the leading of the inward witness. If God speaks something to us as leaders about someone, then it's not because of favoritism. It is because God knows their heart and knows they are willing to obey Him. God is just like any other employer. He doesn't want somebody on the job who's going to fight Him all the time. He wants somebody who is going to do it the way He says when He says to do it. The passage from Brother Hagin's book said, *"Whatever small door He opens for you, walk through it."* I would add to that statement that you should be faithful there and keep studying the WORD so He can open bigger doors of service for you.

A few pages later in the same book, Brother Hagin wrote:

> *"The point is that God richly blesses **obedience**—no matter where you serve Him! God will richly reward you as you walk through the door of service He has opened for you (K. E. Hagin,* Jesus the Open Door *90)."*

In Galatians 5 of the King James Translation, faith is listed as a fruit of the Spirit. However, more modern translations have a word that is closer to the original—faithfulness. We know how faith comes—*by hearing, and hearing by the WORD of God*[157]. So it isn't faith that is a fruit of the Spirit. It is faithfulness—which must be developed over time in relationship with God. When people are coming up the ranks, so to speak, it isn't because the pastor prefers them. It is because God has found them faithful. By the same token, if you are not moving and want to, you better start inventorying your life to see what's in your heart, and if you are faithful according to God's definition of the word. God isn't looking for superstars. He is looking for people He can make into stars—faithful people. What do you want to hear your Father say when you stand before Him? We all want to hear, "Well done! Enter in to the joy of the Lord[158]."

---

[157] Romans 10:17
[158] Matthew 25:21

Don't Compare Doors

> *⁷ And to the angel of the church in Philadelphia write; These things saith he that is holy, he that is true, he that hath the key of David,* **he that openeth, and no man shutteth; and shutteth, and no man openeth;**
>
> *⁸ I know thy works: behold, I have set before thee* **an open door, and no man can shut it***: for thou hast a little strength, and hast kept my word, and hast not denied my name. (Revelation 3:7-8 KJV)*

Jesus said in Revelation 3:8, "I will open doors that no man can shut." But what does He say next? He's going to shut doors and no man can do what to those doors? Open them. Remember, God doesn't have to explain anything to us. He doesn't have to tell us why He opened a particular door or closed it. If He wants to tell us, He will, but He is not obligated to. Besides, we are supposed to be walking by faith[159]. Additionally, Paul warned us in 2 Corinthians 10:12 that it is not wise to compare ourselves to other people. We could easily extend that admonition to include not comparing our assignment with someone else's.

The places God has sent us are just amazing. There is one church we go to in Harcourt, Iowa, that was established by the Swedes. We go there a couple times a year. People often ask us, "How in the world did you get in there?" I don't really know except that years ago, God told us He was going to send us places where others can't get in. At the time, He gave me a strong exhortation to be very wise when I'm there so I don't hurt the people. He said if they start choking on something I'm teaching, then back up and teach on something like the rapture that they can agree with. In other words, get them with me again and then go back and give them a little bit more. In some of those churches, it took three to five years before any gifts of the Spirit manifested. But I never got discouraged because I knew what God told me. And we don't look around and say, "I wonder why He sends Pastor Boudreaux all over the world, and He won't send me to the Carolinas or to Spain?"

---

[159] 2 Corinthians 5:7

CHAPTER 14 – DIFFICULTIES AT THE DOOR

There are times when God will give you a Scripture or a song that just means the world to you when you are going through a trial. Back in 1996, when I was quitting drinking, He did that for me. At that time, I really didn't understand much of what was going on in the spirit realm. I just knew I was shaky and I needed more power to get beyond the alcohol. *Beyond the Open Door*[160] by the Gaither Vocal Band (Band) was that song for me:

> *Beyond the open door is a new and fresh anointing*
> *Hear the Spirit calling you to go*
> *Walk on through the door for the Lord will go before you*
> *Into a greater power you've never known before*
>
> *Beyond the open door is a new and fresh anointing*
> *Hear the Spirit calling you to go*
> *Walk on through the door for the Lord will go before you*
> *Into a greater power you've never known before.*
>
> *(We've included a link to the entire song in the footnotes if you'd like to listen to it yourself.)*

This song was so meaningful because it came at a time when I was spiritually standing at a door into a new room with a greater anointing. But there was a lot of pressure trying to push me back into that old way of thinking and doing. The song helped me understand what was going on in the spirit realm and gave me hope and confidence to go on through the door.

---

[160] http://www.metrolyrics.com/beyond-the-open-door-lyrics-gaither-vocal-band.html

THE ADVERSARIES AT THE OPEN DOOR

Now we've been discussing Revelation 3:7-8 where Jesus told us if He opens a door, then no man can shut it, and if He closes a door, then no man can open it. In my Bible, Revelation 3:8 has a reference marker next to the phrase *open door* pointing to 1 Corinthians 16:9. Let's look at that verse again and see how the two are connected.

> *⁹ For a great door and **effectual is opened unto me**, and there are **many adversaries**. (1 Corinthians 16:9 KJV, footnote mine)*

So there is a door before him that has the capability to produce great effect. But there is also something else there. What is it? Adversaries. Where exactly are those adversaries? They are at those open doors. You must always remember that. Very often when promotion comes, heat comes with it.

When we see the word *many*, most of us think in terms of number or quantity. But there is another way to look at it. *Many* can also mean *different kinds*. In other words, you are being hit with challenges from many different sides and in many different areas of your life. What is the purpose of the adversaries? To try to keep you from going through that open door. Why? Because they know what is on the other side of that open door and they know what will happen if you get over into that room.

How many times have you seen people get saved and start going after God with all they've got? They get hooked into the local body and they are so fired up for God. They are working for God and going after the things of God. Then, all of a sudden, it seems like everything starts coming at them. They don't realize they are at an open door and the things coming against them are trying to stop them from going through it. Most of the time, since they don't know what is going on, they do the only thing they know to do: back up.

The adversaries may come at us fast and furious to keep us from going through that open door. However, there is no need to worry about what is going on, and there is especially no need to back up. We're going to walk right on through the door because the LORD is walking with us. Before we move on, say this out loud, "I'm going through the open door!"

FAMILIAR SPIRITS—SATAN'S RECONNAISSANCE TEAM

Have you ever heard of familiar spirits? What does it mean to you? For some, it may mean one thing, and to others it may mean something else. This is why, if we don't have God's definition of a word, it will either mean nothing to us or it will be very confusing.

Let's come up with a working definition of the term *familiar*[161] *spirits* before we move on. If I am familiar with Christy Christian, what does that mean? Well, it means I know her. I am aware of her thoughts, feelings, and actions on at least some level. Parents are familiar with their children. Wives are familiar with their husbands. In both cases, we know the other one so well, we can often predict what they will say or do in a certain situation, because we know their strengths and weaknesses inside and out.

According to Matthew 18, each one of us has a guardian angel. We don't lose them just because we grow up. The Scripture says, *"Their angel is always before my face*[162].*"* So if God assigns one of His angels to you, then why wouldn't the devil—who always copies and counterfeits God—have a demon assigned to you also? He does, and they are called *familiar spirits*.

One time a guy asked, "Why does this trouble continue on?"

I answered him honestly, "Because it still works."

> *11 Teach me thy way, O LORD, and lead me in a plain path, because of mine enemies. (Psalm 27:11 KJV)*

When you look up the Hebrew meaning of the phrase *mine enemies,* you see it refers to *watchers* (*Brown-Driver-Higgs Hebrew and English Lexicon Unabridged*). Another way to think about watchers would be those who observe. We are New Testament people. So who is our enemy? The devil and his horde. Do we wrestle against flesh and blood? No[163]. Do we hate people? No. We love humanity. One more time, who is your enemy as a New Covenant believer? The devil—Satan—Lucifer.

---

[161] Familiar: Well-known from long or close association; often encountered or experienced, common; having a good knowledge of (Familiar).
[162] Matthew 18:10
[163] Ephesians 6:12

Putting this all together, we begin to understand that a familiar spirit is one who is assigned by the enemy to study and observe a believer to determine all their strengths and weaknesses. Keep in mind, they are not assigned to touch you or hurt you. They are only assigned to follow you and take notes. They are the devil's reconnaissance team. Let me give you some examples to help you better understand how this works.

Christy Christian gets especially irritated when her husband starts griping and complaining about stuff. So Christy's familiar spirit makes a note. Sure enough, every night after work, her husband starts griping and complaining about his work, the house, and the kids. Along similar lines, Billy Believer hates bad attitudes. His familiar spirit knows this well. Therefore, every time Billy goes into Lowe's, Home Depot, or anywhere else, he always runs into someone with a bad attitude.

My particular irritation is traffic. It seems like I'm always getting held up in traffic, or someone burns rubber to get out on the road in front of me, then they slow down to a crawl. I'm behind them shaking my head. "Really? Really? Now you want to drive 20 in a 70?" That's why my wife won't let me put bumper stickers on my vehicles!

Why do these things happen? Believe it or not, the people around us are not the real problem. In each of these cases, familiar spirits arranged these situations because they know exactly what will tick each of us off, cause us to lose our religion, and act the fool.

The amazing part is when you realize they are working so hard on you because you are going through an open door. Suddenly, you can patiently listen to your husband without getting into a fight. You can drive behind the slowpoke and not get hot under the collar. You can even stand in a long line at the store with bad attitudes all around you, and it won't rub off on you. Suddenly, those familiar spirits start looking at their notebooks and scratching their little demon heads saying, "Why isn't this working. It's always worked before."

The purpose of all the stress and chaos is to make you *feel* rejected, to make you *feel* like you have failed, and to make you *think* you are carnal. They hope that you don't know who you are in Christ or how God sees you, so you won't figure out *those lies aren't true*. They hope if they put enough pressure on you, you will back up and never go through that doorway to the greater anointing. Keep in mind, the door is before you for increase and promotion because you have been found faithful. There is no reason to be timid about walking through it.

DOORS FOR PERSONAL GROWTH CAN BE UNCOMFORTABLE

Occasionally, God will send you through some things, not necessarily to help everybody else, but for your benefit alone. There are some quirks, twerks, jerks, and stuff He's trying to get out of you so you don't hurt His people. Peter understood this well.

In Matthew 16 Jesus asked him, "Who do you say that I, the Son of Man, am?"

The other disciples answered, "Well, some say, John the Baptist, some Elijah, and others Jeremiah."

"Okay, but who do you say that I am?" Jesus asked again.

That's when Peter popped off, "Thou art the Christ! The Son of the Living God!" Now if you remember, Jesus called Peter "Petra"—a little rock—after that[164]. But it is amazing, Jesus didn't say He was going to build His church on Peter the man, but rather on the revelation of who he was *in Christ*. All through Peter's writings, you'll see that revelation of being a rock. He refers to building a spiritual house of lively stones[165]. That reference meant something to Peter, and it changed his life forever.

Let's think about this for a minute. Most rocks, when you first pick them up, have a bunch of dirt and jagged edges on them. You have to work with them and rub or scratch on them a while before they start to look good. But then they look really nice and will fit wherever they're needed.

We're like that. Most of us start out with some rough edges on us. Peter, for example, was impulsive and had a bad temper[166]. So, sometimes, God sends us some places to knock some of that rough stuff off. Otherwise, we'd be cutting people. Once it's all done, we're like, "Ah,

---

[164] Matthew 16:13-18 always gets me preaching good in meetings! Glory to God!
[165] 1 Peter 2:5-9
[166] John 18:10-11; 21:7

thank you!" But when we're in the middle of it, we're going, "Ouch! Oooh! Hey, that hurts! Ugh!" and we're just jumping around all over the place.

Look at Peter. He had to go through the experience of rejecting Jesus three times and being restored[167]. But afterwards, he led 3,000 people to Christ on the Day of Pentecost[168]. If you're in the middle of the shaping right now, just remember it will be okay. You're going to look better when you get to the other side of it. In fact, say it right now, "I'm looking better and better in Jesus' name!"

None of us are perfect. But we are way better now than we used to be. We're going somewhere. We don't live condemned. If we have sin[169], then we confess it and ask God to forgive us and cleanse it. At that point, it is over. We cannot let that stuff hold us, and we cannot go back to it. Go forward through the next open door. God will see to it that a door is opened when we are faithful.

CORPORATE DOORWAYS AND CORPORATE ADVERSARIES

Paul wrote to the church at Corinth, and to us, that he didn't want them to be ignorant of what was going on, and of the troubles he had encountered in Asia[170]. He did that because he knew something very important about ministry. Oftentimes, when a man or woman of God begins to go through an open door, those in partnership with them, or those who work closely with them, will go through as well. Yet, there is more to this than simply walking through a door of promotion or increase together. Let's look at 1 Corinthians 16:9 one more time.

> *⁹ For a great door and effectual is opened unto me, and there are **many adversaries**. (1 Corinthians 16:9 KJV)*

---

[167] John 18:15-27 ; 21:15-19

[168] Acts 2:14-41

[169] Some people prefer to say they have a problem or struggle with something. However, everyone must come to understand that if something isn't right, then it isn't just a problem or a struggle. It is sin.

[170] 2 Corinthians 1:8

Chapter 14: Difficulties at the Door

The many adversaries at the open door are why Paul wanted to make sure those around him, his partners in the work of God, understood why there was so much trouble. He understood that when there is trouble, people often start wondering if they are in the will of God or not. You cannot debate the will of God on how well or how poorly something is going. You have to settle it in your heart whether God told you to do it or not. If He did, then no matter what, don't let anything stop you. The gates of hell cannot prevail[171] if you know what God told you, and then you commit to doing it no matter what.

There is one last point I'd like to make about 1 Corinthians 16:9. Paul wrote this letter to an entire church. So not only can individuals go through open doors, but so can a whole body of believers. Brother Hagin taught that the corporate anointing is the strongest anointing there is for this very reason[172]. We must be willing to go through individually, but we must also be willing to go through with our church body when appropriate.

This means that there will be adversaries at those open doors as well trying to stop the entire church body from going through. They know that for those who stick with it and go through the corporate door with their pastors, a new level of revelation and understanding will follow, along with the increase and promotion God has planned because God rewards those who genuinely seek Him[173] and trust Him.

The watchers assigned to that church will know exactly what kind of pressure to bring to stop the most people. For some churches, it may be widespread financial pressure. For others, it may be marriages and families under attack or strife in general. What you will see is that some people will go boldly through and overcome, but many may not. If that happens, those who do not may struggle along for a while, but eventually they succumb to the enemy's pressure and leave the church. This is

---

[171] Matthew 16:18
[172] You can read more about the corporate anointing in Chapter 15 of *Understanding the Anointing* by Kenneth E. Hagin.
[173] Hebrews 11:6

different from God moving someone to a new church. These moves are people taking things into their own hands and escaping.

CHAPTER 15 – MINISTRY ROOMS AND PHASES

Through Paul's revelation, we understand that once Jesus died and rose again, He was no longer the *body* of Christ. At that time, those who accepted the free gift of salvation became the Body of Christ and He became the *Head* of the Body of Christ[174].

First Corinthians 12 tells us there is only one Body, but there are a whole bunch of members. We know that Jesus was the first begotten of the dead[175], but not the last. There have been a whole bunch of us since then. We, all together, make up the Body of Christ. No one person has it all or has the Spirit without measure. This is why there is so much more power available to the corporate body. Each one brings their part and it combines to make the full and complete Body[176] with an unlimited measure of the Spirit. Whether you realize it or not, I need the grace of God on you and I need you to be faithful. You need the same from me and every other member of the Body of Christ.

MINISTRY GIFTS AND THE IMPORTANCE OF A SHEPHERD

*⁷ But unto every one of us is given **grace** according to **the measure of the gift of Christ**. ⁸ Wherefore he saith, When he ascended up on high, he led captivity captive, and **gave gifts unto men**. (Ephesians 4:7-8 KJV)*

The grace in verse 7 is the grace for service (*Thayer's Greek Lexicon*). Paul goes on to explain the gifts Jesus gave in verse 11.

*¹¹ And he gave **some, apostles**; and some, **prophets**; and some, **evangelists**; and some, **pastors** and **teachers**; ¹² For*

---

[174] 1 Corinthians 12:27; Colossians 1:18
[175] Revelation 1:5; Romans 8:29
[176] Ephesians 4:16

***the perfecting of the saints, for the work of the ministry, for the edifying of the body of Christ**: (Ephesians 4:11-12 KJV)*

That little tiny word *some* is so very important. Keep it in mind as we go through the rest of this chapter. Why did Christ give these gifts to men? Verse 12 lists three stated purposes:
1. *for the perfecting of the saints*
2. *for the work of the ministry*
3. *for the edifying of the Body of Christ*

Now John 3:34 tells us that Jesus had the Spirit without measure. So when He walked on Earth, He was the *body* of Christ. He was completely limitless concerning the Spirit of God and He walked in all five of the ministry gifts. However, when He prepared to leave, He said, "I am not going to take these gifts with me. I have to leave these ministry gifts on Earth, so I will give them to mankind[177]."

Many have gotten confused and think just because they have Jesus as their LORD and Savior that they have a shepherd[178]. Let's pause here and think through this carefully. Jesus is no longer physically here on Planet Earth. He did not take the Office of the Shepherd with Him when He left. Neither did He take the other four gifts with Him. According to Ephesians 4:8, He gave them to men.

People love to quote Psalm 23 as proof that Jesus is our shepherd, but He cannot be our shepherd here on Earth. Let's look at what Jesus thought about this:

> *36 But when he saw the multitudes, he was moved with compassion on them, because **they fainted**, and **were scattered abroad**, as **sheep having no shepherd**. (Matthew 9:36 KJV)*

Why was Jesus moved with compassion? Because the multitudes had no shepherd. It is important to note here that Jesus wasn't moved with compassion because they had no apostle, no prophet, or no TV evangelist.

---

[177] Keep in mind, in Ephesians 4:8 the word *men* means mankind. Jesus did not leave these gifts specifically to males (444.anthropos - Helps Word Studies).

[178] In the Bible, pastors are often referred to as shepherds.

He was moved with compassion specifically because they had no shepherd.

What happens when people don't have a shepherd? They faint and get scattered abroad. In other words, they quit going after the things of God. They get tired of pursuing and start slowing up or give up altogether. Scattering means things go in all different directions. It implies chaos. We do not want our health to be scattered. We do not want our marriage to be scattered. When you work hard to be faithful to God and have received the benefits of that faithfulness, you do not want them scattered. I want to obey Proverbs 13:22 and leave an inheritance for my kids and my grandkids.

Jesus no longer lives here. His plan was for us to have a pastor here to help guide and feed us, and to keep us from fainting and getting scattered. For my wife and me, Sally is the pastor of our church, so that means she is my pastor.

People confuse going to church with being saved. You can be saved anywhere. You can be out in the woods on a tree stump and ask Jesus Christ into your life and get saved. But that doesn't make you a shepherd. You can't shepherd yourself. You need a shepherd so your life will stay right. Then you need to plug into a local church because that is how God said to do it and we want to be faithful[179].

I'll say it again: You don't have to go to church to be saved, but we want more out of this life than just waiting around to get to heaven. We don't want to just be saved and then be scattered. We want to be saved, be victorious, be growing, and be strong. Glory to God! I want to look so much better that people will come by and say, "Ricky? Is that you? You're still alive?"

MINISTRY PHASES AND ROOMS

In the natural, if you go into your kitchen, what kind of equipment are you likely to find there? Most people will have a stove, a refrigerator, a sink, some pots and pans, and the like. What if you go into the bedroom?

---

[179] Hebrews 10:25

Well, the equipment will be different. You'll have a bed, a nightstand, a lamp, a dresser, and such. Is all of this equipment in the same house? Sure it is. It is just in different rooms because it is used for different purposes.

We can see through the Scriptures that there are phases and rooms in both the fivefold ministry offices and the other ministries within the Body of Christ. In each phase of ministry, there are usually several different rooms. In each room, we will have different equipment to help us with that phase of ministry.

In Kenneth E. Hagin's book *I Believe in Visions*, he shared about the different phases of his ministry (first, second, third, and fourth). Each of the phases had to do with faithfulness. In that same book, Brother Hagin also shared about a time when Jesus told him he had been unfaithful concerning the first phase of his ministry because he would not do what God had asked him to do. Following is an excerpt from this book. When you read it, I want you to keep in mind everything we have been learning about faithfulness. At this point, the language Jesus used should mean more to you:

> *Jesus told me that, even as He had appeared to my mother before I was born and had told her, "Fear not, the child will be born," that I would minister in the power of the Spirit and would fulfill the ministry He has called me to.*
>
> *Then, He talked to me about the last church that I had pastored, saying that at that time, February of 1949, I had entered into the first phase of my ministry. He said, "Some ministers I have called to the ministry live and die without getting into even the first phase of the ministry I have for them." Jesus added that this is one reason why many ministers die prematurely—they are living only in His permissive will.*
>
> *For 15 years, I had only been in His permissive will*[180]...

Chapter 15: Ministry Rooms and Phases

*Then He talked about the time **I entered into the first phase of my ministry in 1949**. He said I had been **unfaithful** and I hadn't done what He told me to do; I hadn't told the people what He told me to tell them. I answered, "Lord, I wasn't unfaithful. I did obey You. I left my church, and I went out on the evangelistic field."*

"Yes," He said, "you left the church and went out into evangelistic work. But, you didn't do what I told you to do. The reason you didn't is because you doubted it was my Spirit who had spoken to you. You see, faith obeys my Word whether it is the written Word of God or My Spirit who has spoken unto man."

I fell down before Him saying, "Yes, Lord, I have failed and I am sorry." I repented with many tears because I had missed His will and had doubted His dealings with me.

*"Stand up on your feet," He said. As I stood before Him again, He told me that I had entered into the **second** phase of my ministry in January of 1950, and at that time, He had spoken to me by prophecy and by the still small voice in my heart. In the next eight months, during this second phase of my ministry, I had believed, I had been faithful, and I had obeyed.*

*Now, I was to enter into the **third** phase. He said **if I would be faithful to what He told me**—if I would believe and obey Him—He would appear to me again. At that time I would enter into the **fourth** and final phase of my ministry. (K. E. Hagin,* Visions *46-47)*

Isn't that last paragraph interesting? It was never about whether Jesus wanted to appear to Brother Hagin again. It was contingent on if Brother Hagin would be faithful to do what he was told to do. I remember when Brother Hagin was in his fourth and final phase. He said the LORD challenged him in 1994 to quit having *All Faith Crusades* and to go back to the local church and have *Holy Ghost Meetings*. We went to several of them over the years. They were amazing. Sometimes, Holy Ghost laughter would break out all over the place.

I calculated this one day and realized that Brother Hagin went into the ministry around 1934. He had been in ministry, working for God, 15 years before he ever entered the first phase of what God had planned for him. When I was at Rhema, he used to tell us that he fought more devils in the eight months following that transition to the first phase of his ministry than he had the entire previous 15 years.

Similarly, Paul studied under the famous rabbi Gamaliel for approximately 15 years before he ever got into the first phase of the ministry God had planned for him. Once he jumped in, devils followed him all over the place trying to stop him[181]. That's interesting, isn't it? Paul and Brother Hagin both went into some hard places as soon as they stepped through the open door. But they both stayed faithful to the course because they had built their trust in God by years of following the Holy Ghost in all things small and big. So don't be in a hurry to jump ahead. Let God mold you and make you so you will be able to stay in His perfect will and not just His permissive will.

Now when Brother Hagin talks about Jesus calling him unfaithful, it means more to us. We understand better what Jesus meant. Brother Hagin hadn't done something he was told to do. Therefore, he was qualified as unfaithful. Faith obeys the WORD, whether written or by the Spirit because all believers have the same inward witness. But notice, moving into the fourth and final phase of his ministry was not contingent upon God. It was dependent upon Brother Hagin's faithfulness. Of course, we know now that in June of 1979 he entered that final phase of ministry. Then he was with us until 2003 when he took off and went to be with the LORD.

ALL MINISTRIES HAVE PHASES AND ROOMS

Earlier we established that every believer has a place in the Body of Christ, and we now understand the ministry gifts God gave to the Church

Chapter 15: Ministry Rooms and Phases

to strengthen, equip, and edify it. We also saw, through Brother Hagin's writing how fivefold ministry gifts have rooms and phases.

> *²⁸ And God hath set some in the church, first **apostles**, secondarily **prophets**, thirdly **teachers**, after that **miracles**, then **gifts of healings**, **helps**, **governments**, **diversities of tongues**. (1 Corinthians 12:28 KJV)*

While the ministry gifts listed in verse 28 are not the same as the offices listed in Ephesians 4:11-12, they are, nevertheless, ministries within the Body of Christ. So if the fivefold ministry can have rooms and phases, then so can these other ministries.

See, I know where I am: the third phase and third room. The second room of this third phase was a room that had many miracles in it. Then, about a year and a half ago, the LORD began to deal with me and said, "You're going to go into the third phase. In this room, there will be such revelation and teaching as you've never known."

Now understand that when you enter a new phase or a new room, you don't lose the other stuff. A new emphasis is added. When you are faithful to that and will do that, you will always get the highest flow and increase will always come. However, as increase comes, don't leave the WORD which brought the increase to serve the increase. Let's take a look at Acts 6 to see what I mean:

> *And in those days, when the number of the disciples was multiplied, there arose a murmuring of the Grecians against the Hebrews, because their widows were neglected in the daily ministration.*
>
> *² Then the twelve called the multitude of the disciples unto them, and said, It is not reason that we should leave the word of God, and serve tables.*
>
> *³ Wherefore, brethren, look ye out among you seven men of honest report, full of the Holy Ghost and wisdom, whom we may appoint over this business.*

> *⁴ But we will give ourselves continually to prayer, and to the ministry of the word. (Acts 6:1-4 KJV)*

The new Church had been faithful and was standing at an open door of increase. They had to decide if they were going to walk through it together, or if they were going to let the strife, which the adversaries were sending, tear them apart. Luckily for us, they decided to go through it together. They wisely decided the twelve could not leave the WORD to serve the increase it had brought.

It works the same in our personal lives. If we don't have much, and we are following after God, it seems easy to go to church two or three times a week. But as prosperity begins to come and we get a toy or two, suddenly it becomes more difficult to get to church on Sunday. We must realize, God didn't give us that boat or that house on the lake so we could start missing Sundays. He didn't give us that increase of additional businesses or that promotion at work so we would be so tired or so busy on Wednesday evenings that we can't come either.

I'm talking about a continual increase. I don't want to hit a ceiling or tap out. I want to go all the way and be like Paul and say, "I have finished my course. I have kept the faith[182]." Another way to say that is, "I have kept the WORD God gave me." That's why he wrote, "Examine yourselves to see whether or not you are in the faith[183]." He was talking about the specific WORD God gave *you*. That is what Jesus was talking about when He told Brother Hagin he had been unfaithful. He hadn't stuck to the WORD he was given. He hadn't done what he was told to do.

Let's continue in Acts 6:

> *⁵ And the saying pleased the whole multitude: and they chose **Stephen**, a man full of faith and of the Holy Ghost, and **Philip**, and Prochorus, and Nicanor, and Timon, and Parmenas, and Nicolas a proselyte of Antioch:*
>
> *⁶ Whom they set before the apostles: and when they had prayed, they laid their hands on them.*

---

[182] 2 Timothy 4:7
[183] 2 Corinthians 13:5

Chapter 15: Ministry Rooms and Phases

> *⁷ **And the word of God increased**; and the number of the disciples multiplied in Jerusalem greatly; and a great company of the priests were obedient to the faith.*
>
> *⁸ And Stephen, full of faith and power, did great wonders and miracles among the people. (Acts 6:5-8 KJV)*

The increase of teaching the WORD brought the people. But the apostles realized they couldn't neglect the WORD to wait on the people, otherwise, they would start moving backward. In other words, they couldn't stop preaching the WORD to serve the increase that had come as a result of preaching the WORD.

We see here that Stephen and Philip were chosen as some of the faithful men to take over the distribution to the widows. If we look at verse 2 in the Amplified, we get a better idea of what they were dealing with:

> *² So the Twelve [apostles] convened the multitude of the disciples and said, It is not seemly or desirable or right that we should have to give up or neglect [preaching] the Word of God in order to attend **to serving at tables** and **superintending the distribution of food**. (Acts 6:2 AMPC)*

From this is it very easy to see that Stephen and Philip started out in the Ministry of Helps as waiters handing out food. They didn't start out as apostles or evangelists. They started out serving food to women. There are phases and rooms in every ministry. That was the first phase of their ministry. Let's look and see where they ended up:

> *⁸ And Stephen, full of faith and **power**, did great **wonders** and **miracles among the people**. (Acts 6:5-8 KJV)*

> *⁵ Then Philip went down to the city of Samaria, and **preached Christ** unto them.*
>
> *⁶ And the people with one accord gave heed unto those things which Philip spake, hearing and seeing **the miracles which he did.***

> *⁷ For unclean spirits, crying with loud voice, came out of many that were possessed with them: and many taken with palsies, and that were lame, were healed.*
>
> *⁸ And there was great joy in that city. (Acts 8:5-8 KJV)*

So we can see that these men did not stay in the Ministry of Helps permanently. They were no longer waiting on tables. But I think we can all agree that neither of them would have refused to wait on tables if God told them to do it again. A humble person will stay humble even as they progress through the phases and rooms of ministry. If humility is lost, progression will stop. So don't be afraid or stubborn about helping out.

One of the things my wife and I have always tried to do is jump in and help alongside our Ministry of Helps any time we ask them to do something. Most of the time, they will tell us, "Y'all don't do that."

"We can help you."

"Yes, Sir, we know you can," they'll answer. "But we want to honor the office higher than us. We've got this. Don't be concerned about it at all."

At least they know we are not above helping. We don't mind helping at all. We know how to work hard. But if you start humble, then you should stay humble, and live humble too.

Stephen and Philip weren't opposed to waiting tables. They didn't say, "Oh no! I'm above that now, because I flow in the power of God and I've had miracles." Are you kidding me? They wouldn't have power and miracles if they had that kind of attitude. They stayed faithful.

> *⁸ And the next day we that were of Paul's company departed and came unto Caesarea: and we entered into the house of **Philip the evangelist, which was one of the seven**; and abode with him. (Acts 21:8 KJV)*

Here we see that Philip has gone from being *one of the seven* waiters in Acts 6 to an *evangelist*. Brother Hagin taught that Philip is the only one in the Bible we can study as a pattern for a true evangelist. If someone says they are an evangelist, then they need to study Philip's life. According to Romans 12:8, evangelists are exhorters. They easily exhort people to get saved. As we study Philip, though, we see he could exhort people to

Chapter 15: Ministry Rooms and Phases

salvation *and do many miracles*[184]. This is a key for true evangelists. If they don't have the gift of miracles, then they are not true evangelists. They are exhorters.

Staying on this same subject, let's turn our attention to Barnabas and Saul.

> *¹Now there were in the church that was at Antioch certain **prophets** and **teachers**; as Barnabas, and Simeon that was called Niger, and Lucius of Cyrene, and Manaen, which had been brought up with Herod the tetrarch, and Saul.*
>
> *² As they ministered to the Lord, and fasted, the Holy Ghost said, **Separate me Barnabas and Saul for the work** whereunto I have called them. (Acts 13:1-2 KJV)*

According to this passage, Barnabas and Saul were separated out for an assignment by God. We also know that everyone listed in verse 1 was either a prophet, teacher, or a prophet-teacher. I believe Paul (here called Saul) was a prophet-teacher because of the amount of instructing he did throughout his ministry.

> *¹⁴ Which when **the apostles, Barnabas and Paul**, heard of, they rent their clothes, and ran in among the people, crying out. (Acts 14:14 KJV)*

Obviously, some time has passed between Acts 13 and Acts 14. Who are *the apostles* now? Barnabas and Paul. So they have received a promotion. There is always increase when you are found faithful.

---

[184] Acts 8:6

Faithfulness

CHAPTER 16 – MORE ABOUT THE ANOINTING

A TASTE OF YOUR FUTURE

Sometimes God will let you taste your future. It is not teasing, but a taste of what is to come. Let me explain with an example Brother Kenneth Hagin shared frequently. In his book, *Understanding the Anointing*, Brother Hagin shares a story from September of 1970 when he and Sister Oretha, his wife, were up in Buffalo, New York, doing a meeting. You can find it briefly mentioned in the section titled "That Stronger Anointing" (K. E. Hagin, *Anointing* 37-38) but there is also a more detailed account in a very old article he wrote titled *First Things First* on Scribd.com (K. E. Hagin 1st Things). When we were students at Rhema, he would often share this story when he was teaching on the anointing.

In 1970, he didn't have crusade people traveling with him. One night he was carrying in the last box of books for their book table into their room at the Holiday Inn. He said he began to feel very ill as he was coming into the room. This thing just overwhelmed him. He positioned himself so that if he fainted he would fall across the bed, which he did. Sister Oretha came running, saying, "Ken! Ken! Are you all right?" because it had been a decade or so since she saw him sick.

"Honey, I'm sick big," he replied. "I'm sick as a horse[185]."

They began to seek God immediately because he had never missed a meeting in all his years of ministry. He said, "I'm going to have to miss this meeting if I don't get better." In fact, when we were in school, he told us he thought he would have had to get better to die! I'm not kidding, that's exactly what he said.

---

[185] For those that might not understand this Texas colloquialism, horses are big; so, he meant he was very sick.

Faithfulness

As they were seeking God and praying about it, He told them, "Close this meeting out and go back to Tulsa, Oklahoma, and have a week-long meeting. When you do, the anointing of God that you have experienced only four times in the past twenty years will now come upon you to abide." God then healed him and raised him as he went obediently to close out the meeting and prepare to go back to Tulsa.

David wrote, *"Oh taste and see that the LORD is good" (Psalm 34:8a KJV)*. At times, God will let you taste of your future. As I said above, He is not teasing you. It is a glimpse of what is ahead of you to spur you along. Over the course of those 20 years, God had allowed Brother Hagin to taste his future because of his hunger for more of God and an increase in God's power flowing through him. Brother Hagin shared that once he had tasted that greater anointing he craved it and longed for it, but he said he never could get it to show up when he wanted it. It was only as God would will.

Maybe you've had an anointing come on you that was so different or so powerful it left you wondering, "What can I do to get that back? It is so powerful. It is so strong." Many times, that is yet into your future. If you so badly want it back, then stay faithful and a day will come when you will walk in it. That's why God told Brother Hagin, "The anointing that you've experienced only four times in the past twenty years will now come upon you to abide." And it did! That's when the tangible anointing was given for certain things and that was increase tied to faithfulness, not to diligence or hard work.

Even though I've told you this story, I want you to read it exactly the way he wrote it in his book *Understanding the Anointing*, because there are a few more things I want to bring out about it:

> *In September 1970, while my wife and I were in New York State, the Lord instructed me to return to Tulsa and hold a seminar. Our offices then were in Brother T. L. Osborn's old office building on North Utica. We had a little chapel in there that would seat 300, so we'd hold a seminar now and then. The Lord told me to have a Healing Seminar at night and a Prayer Seminar in the mornings from*

Chapter 16: More About the Anointing

> *October 11–18, 1970. He said, "Teach on intercessory prayer." (Those messages were later made into the book* The Interceding Christian.*)*
>
> *He told me what to teach on in every service. "When you come to Wednesday night," He said, "speak on special ministries and special anointings. Relate your experience of what I said to you twenty years ago when I appeared to you, and then lay hands on the people. "And when you lay hands on them, that stronger anointing that has come on you four times in the last twenty years will come to abide.* ***This will be a new beginning for you.*** *You see, you've never done what you should have done with the healing ministry." (K. E. Hagin,* Understanding the Anointing *140-141)[emphasis mine]*

Brother Hagin had been in ministry 30 years at that point, yet the Lord told him that night would be a new beginning for him in the ministry. Along similar lines, back in 1996 God told us, "I have opened a door for you and that is why change is coming." You see, I had traveled and pastored for several years, and we pretty much thought that we were going to continue along those lines. We weren't sure what was coming next, because God doesn't tell us everything. Yet, even though He doesn't tell us everything in our future, He does give us glimpses of our future.

THE PERSONAL ANOINTING VS. ANOINTING FOR MINISTRY

In order to fully understand how rooms and phases of ministry work, it is extremely important to understand the types of grace. Many have confused saving grace with serving grace. There is a grace of God that will save all of humanity[186]. That is a favor that is granted to all humanity with nothing required other than believing Jesus died and rose again. But there is also a grace, or an ability of God, that will come upon a man or a woman for service to God and humanity. It requires faith to get into it[187].

---

[186] Ephesians 2:8-9
[187] Romans 5:2

This is why both Peter and James taught if you humble yourselves and do what God asks, He will give you more grace[188]. They were talking about grace to serve the Body of Christ. It is a greater degree of anointing that comes by faithfulness.

Faithfulness is independent of anointing. But Christians today should have a clear understanding of the anointing and how it works. In his book *Understanding the Anointing,* Brother Kenneth E. Hagin gives an excellent description of the difference between the personal anointing (the anointing within) and the anointing for ministry (the anointing upon):

> *Every born-again, Spirit-filled believer has a measure of the Spirit and anointing within, 1 John 2:27 says, but this "personal anointing" never will be increased. There's nothing in the Scripture that indicates you can have a double portion of your personal anointing.*
>
> *Yes, Elisha had a double portion of what Elijah had, but that was an anointing to minister. (K. E. Hagin,* Understanding the Anointing *135)*

Since he referenced 1 John 2:27, let's look at it also:

> *²⁷ But the anointing which ye have received of him* **abideth in you***, and ye need not that any man teach you: but as the same anointing teacheth you of all things, and is truth, and is no lie, and even as it hath taught you, ye shall abide in him. (1 John 2:27 KJV)*

I believe we can all agree that the anointing this verse refers to is the anointing **within** every born-again believer. I believe we can also agree that a teacher is one of the fivefold ministry gifts[189]. It is very important that we understand what he is and is not saying in 1 John 2:27. First, he is not saying, "Don't ever be taught by a man." He's saying that a man or a woman under the anointing can teach. He's showing us this is the anointing within. Every born-again believer has the anointing within.

---

[188] 1 Peter 5:6; James 4:6-10
[189] Ephesians 4:11

Chapter 16: More About the Anointing

*²⁷ And it shall come to pass in that day, that **his burden shall be taken away from off thy shoulder**, and his yoke from off thy neck, and **the yoke shall be destroyed because of the anointing**. (Isaiah 10:27 KJV)*

When we look carefully at this verse, we see that there is no distinction made as to which type of anointing removes burdens and destroys yokes. It clearly says *the anointing*. So when you study the Scriptures, the anointing within or the personal anointing will begin to reveal things to you. As that revelation comes, things can be removed and destroyed from your life just as surely as when hands are laid on a fellow brother or sister because it is the same anointing.

Now with that understanding about the anointing within, let's look again at what Brother Hagin had to say about the anointing:

Every born-again, Spirit-filled believer has a measure of the Spirit and anointing within, 1 John 2:27 says, but this "personal anointing" never will be increased. There's nothing in the Scripture that indicates you can have a double portion of your personal anointing.

Yes, Elisha had a double portion of what Elijah had, but that was an anointing to minister. (K. E. Hagin,
Understanding the Anointing *135)*

This reference to Elisha and the double portion is found in 2 Kings 2:9. We must think carefully here. Elisha could not have been referring to a double portion of the anointing within, because they did not have the anointing ***withi***, since Christ had not come, been crucified, and resurrected. At that time, the Holy Spirit came only ***upon*** the prophets, priests, and kings to help them fulfill their office. That is the anointing upon for service to the kingdom of God.

DON'T SHIPWRECK YOUR FAITH

It is within humanity to increase. It is God-given. It is in us to excel. It is in us to produce. These things are already in us and given to us from God. Everything about God is always multiplying, growing, and accelerating. Even though the desire to increase, produce, and multiply is God-given, we must be very careful not to let our desires overwhelm the process. Here's the problem: If you get out too far ahead of God, it can cause you to shipwreck your faith[190].

God will often tell a minister to go to a certain country on a certain date. When He does that, it means He has prepared the way and everything is now ready for that minister to do his work. However, if that minister gets too excited about the mission and decides he would rather go two weeks earlier, the field may not be prepared. The work could fail. Or, even worse, the minister could find himself in a very hostile and dangerous situation where he gets physically hurt. At the very least, he is going to leave there with his faith shaken. Those who helped him get there might even have their faith rattled about it all too. This is why it is so important that we trust God enough to do what He says when He says to do it.

God is smarter than we are. I want to be found faithful so I can have the power required to minister to anyone who comes to one of my meetings. Let me explain.

Years ago, we were holding a meeting in Lockhart, Texas, down by Austin. It was sometime in the early 2000s. I don't remember the exact date, but we were talking about the definition of the word *maimed*[191].

> *43 And if thy hand offend thee, cut it off: it is better for thee to enter into life **maimed**, than having two hands to go into hell, into the fire that never shall be quenched: (Mark 9:43 KJV)*

Please understand, Jesus wasn't literally talking about hurting the physical body; rather, He was emphasizing the importance of the situation so He used the word *maimed* for body parts. As I was ministering, the LORD said, "There is someone here maimed. Call that out." I did so immediately, and a lady came forward who had lost a finger. I mean it was gone.

---

[190] Proverbs 28:20

[191] Maim: to deprive of the use of some part of the body by wounding or the like; cripple (maimed)

Chapter 16: More About the Anointing

I did what He said and I ministered to her. While I was ministering to her, the finger grew out to the second joint. It did not fully go to the third joint. People were shouting, dancing, and running all over the place. But I was perplexed and wondered why we didn't get the whole finger. I was excited about the two joints, but we didn't get the whole finger.

Later, when I got back to the room, I began to ask God about it. "How come we didn't get that whole finger?"

He answered, "Because there isn't enough power of Mine flowing through you yet. It is a progression because there are degrees of an anointing. But if you will stay faithful, and if you do what My Spirit tells you to do, a day will come when I will release that into your life and you will see fingers and arms grow out. But it takes time." I'm hungry for it. That's why I keep after this. I'm hungry. It's our job to be hungry, and it is God's job to feed us.

Remember that morning in New Mexico when God came in the cab of my truck and said, "You've been bugging me about the greater anointing to see the miraculous, to see the limbs grow, and other signs and wonders. You have to understand, once I release that, I cannot take it back." Then He quoted Romans 11:29, "For *the gifts and calling of God are without repentance.*"

He went on to say, "If I, through a process of time, give you tests of obedience and you do them, then I learn that I can trust you. Along the same lines, with every test of obedience, you can learn to trust Me in greater measures. Then, once you get to a certain place, that stronger power—that stronger anointing—will no longer work against you. It will work for you."

Let me quickly explain a few things about how the increase of the anointing can work against you. Jack Coe was a mighty man of God[192]. After Brother Jack had passed, Brother Hagin told the Rhema students publicly about a dinner he had with Oral Roberts. Now remember, Brother Hagin and Brother Roberts were good friends. During that dinner, Brother Roberts mentioned he had recently received a phone call from Jack Coe around one or two o'clock in the morning. Brother Jack wanted to tell him

---

[192] http://healingandrevival.com/BioJCoe.htm

that he had a new addition added to his tent and it was now bigger than Brother Roberts' tent by about 3,000 seats. Brother Jack's new tent was supposed to seat about 30,000 people. It is important to understand, this tent addition and the resulting phone call were about competition.

As I meditated on that one day, the LORD asked me, "Did you notice, after that tent expansion, the increase of the anointing no longer worked for him [Jack Coe]? Indeed, it began to work against him." You see, God used him powerfully, but he died when he was only 38 years old. Then the LORD went on to tell me, "If you follow the process and don't jump out ahead of it, when you get there, you can stay there."

King Saul couldn't keep the spoils of war with the Amalekites or stay in his office, because he had become unfaithful to do what God would ask. God's desire is to bless His kids and prosper them in all areas of their lives. But the only way He can do that is if we are faithful to trust Him and do what He asks when He asks. The BLESSING never operates without faith and faithfulness.

CHAPTER 17 - FINAL THOUGHTS

If you are like me, you probably realize you haven't always done everything God asked you to do in the way He asked you to do it. We cannot live in that place of regret. We have to learn from those mistakes and say, "I'm going to do better now."

I am so grateful for the following scripture:

> *12 And I thank Christ Jesus our Lord, who hath enabled me, for that he counted me **faithful**, putting me **into the ministry** (1 Timothy 1:12 KJV)*

Now, what did Paul say God counted him? Faithful. Where did he put faithful Paul? Into the ministry. Say this aloud, "I am glad, I am faithful." If you are reading this book, then you are faithful in at least some areas and most likely you want to become faithful in more. It takes faithfulness to willingly sit down and read a book this size. I believe this means you want to be one whose pastor doesn't feel the need to double-check on you once you agree to help him with something. You may not be where you want to be just yet, but remember you are a good help and you are growing in faithfulness.

As you listen and obey the voice of the Holy Ghost and grow in faithfulness, always remember that God does not have to explain Himself. When you come into those times where you don't understand why He is asking you to do something, remember He always has a purpose and, therefore, you can trust Him. You might not know what that purpose is right now, but someday you probably will.

Faithfulness brings you to the open door. Beyond the open door is an increased anointing. This is why "to whom much is given, much will be required[193]." As we grow, we're ready.

There was a time when I was chomping at the bit to get going. I was constantly asking God if it was time yet. I asked a thousand times if I

---

[193] Luke 12:48

asked once. Finally, it was time. I held back a moment and said, "Oh, I'm not sure if I'm quite ready yet." So, let God lead you by His Spirit. Don't try to force anything, especially a door that is not open. Let Jesus open doors because you have been found faithful.

We know there are many adversaries at the open door hoping to get us to back up. If we wait for Jesus to open the door, then we know we are ready to go on through and the adversaries can't touch us. But if we force the door, then we may not be ready to deal with them and we may get pushed back quite far.

WE MUST FAITHFULLY CONTINUE UNTIL JESUS RETURNS

I believe we can all agree that we are getting closer to the return of Jesus than we've ever been before. I grew up in the Assemblies of God. Back then, adults were always telling us, "You better be ready. You better be ready tonight." I'm sure some of you reading this book have heard the same thing. In fact, Peter told us they had the same trouble back then with people scoffing and saying, "Really? Where is this coming? You've said for years that Jesus is coming[194]."

My birthday is in August. In 2017, I turned 60. So I could say with confidence then that we are 60 years closer to Jesus' return than when I was born. He hasn't come yet, but we are assured He will return[195]. I believe He is coming soon. I live every day as if He is coming tonight. But when it comes to doing the work I've been assigned, I work as if it will be several years before He returns. We cannot just sit down and wait for Him to come. We must be busy about the Master's business until He does come[196].

We know His coming is soon, and the catching away will happen very quickly when He does. But there is work yet to be done. Part of our personal commission is to encourage the saints of God to continue doing

---

[194] 2 Peter 3:3
[195] Matthew 16:27; 24:4-5; 30-31, 40-44; 25:1-2, 13, 31-36; Mark 8:38; Luke 12:37-40; John 14:1-3; Acts 1:11; 2 Thessalonians 2:1-2; Hebrews 9:28; Revelation 16:15
[196] Matthew 25:14-30

Chapter 17: Final Thoughts

the work of the ministry[197]. We want to encourage people to continue to stay steady and be faithful. One of the greatest things that will bless a pastor concerning the flock God has put him over is to see people faithfully continuing in the things God has asked them to do.

The Bible tells us that faithfulness is a rare quality[198]. At this time, in the world as a whole, it appears faithfulness to anything is sorely lacking. People have become lackadaisical[199]. A perfect example of this is when a new piece of technology comes out like an iPhone. When it first comes out, people are lined up for days trying to get it. But then, not even a year later, something newer comes along and they're ready to trash the old one and stand in line for days again to get the newest one. Every time, I am amazed at how quickly someone can go from thinking something is the greatest to thinking it is just mundane[200].

This life is like that. For example, you're going to have to figure out that in a marriage, it is going to be the same thing over and over. You're going to get up. Your wife will be right there beside you. You're going to have to brush your teeth and comb your hair. If you've got little ones, you're going to have to get them up and dressed. You have to feed everyone and get them out of the house for work and school. It is just a continuous circle. But it should never become so mundane to us that we aren't excellent at it or faithful to it any longer. Our walk with Jesus is the same every day. Get up. Read the WORD. Do the WORD. Pray in the Holy Ghost. Every day—over and over again—we must be continual and faithful in the things of God.

---

[197] Titus 4:5
[198] Psalm 12:1; Proverbs 20:6; Philippians 2:19-22
[199] Lacking vitality and purpose: lazy or idle—especially in a dreamy way (Lackadaisical).
[200] Common, ordinary, banal, unimaginative (Mundane).

CONFESSION OF FAITHFULNESS

Dear Father, thank You for loving me, helping me, directing me, guiding me, and protecting me by the Holy Ghost in light of the WORD.

So thank You, Father, I am faithful. That means whatever You have in Your heart is what I have in mine. I will do it the way You say to do it. I'll not add to or take away from it. I won't change it. When You tell me, I will be quick to obey. I'll not question why. I'll trust You and do it the way You have it in Your heart.

As I obey You, increase will come my way. In Jesus' name.

APPENDIX 1 – THE PLAN OF SPIRITUAL SALVATION

Sin is falling short of God's standard and the Bible tells us that everyone has fallen short[201]. The Bible is also very clear that the payment for sin is spiritual death[202] or eternal separation from God the Father and from love. Let me assure you God does not want to be separated from a single human being. There is no sin too great for Him to forgive if we'll just ask.

Jesus said there is only one way to the Father and it is through Him.

> *6 Jesus saith unto him, I am the way, the truth, and the life: no man cometh unto the Father, but by me. (John 14:6 KJV)*

Why would Jesus say that? He didn't say that because God is trying to limit who gets into heaven. Quite the contrary, He said it because sin demands death and God loves each of us so much that He sent His own Son to die in our place.

> *16 "For this is how God loved the world: He gave his one and only Son, so that everyone who believes in him will not perish but have eternal life. 17 God sent his Son into the world not to judge the world, but to save the world through him. (John 3:16-17 NLT)*

> *8 But God showed his great love for us by sending Christ to die for us while we were still sinners. (Romans 5:8, NLT)*

Imagine that you are a criminal and you are at court. The judge has found you guilty of a capital crime and has pronounced the death sentence. But the gavel is still in the air; it hasn't hit the desk yet. In walks a man—

---

200 Romans 3:23
202 Romans 6:23

Faithfulness

just a regular looking man—who says, "Judge, I know he's guilty, but I'll take his place. Forgive him and set him free. Wipe his slate clean." That's what Jesus did for us.

The judge is looking at you and waiting for your answer to see if you will accept this man's offer of grace and of salvation. Will you?

The apostle Paul told us in Romans 10:9 and 10 that all you have to do is call out to Jesus, confess Him as LORD of your life, believe in your heart that God raised Him from the dead, and you'll be saved spiritually or born again.

If you accept His offer and call out to Him by faith, you will be saved. The Judge will not condemn you.

> *¹This means that anyone who belongs to Christ has become a new person. The old life is gone; a new life has begun! (Romans 8:1 NKJV)*

It doesn't matter how simple the prayer, the very moment a person cries out to Jesus by faith for spiritual salvation, we believe one of the most amazing *instant* miracles of transformation occurs. Their spirit is made brand-new.

> *¹⁷ This means that anyone who belongs to Christ has become a new person. The old life is gone; a new life has begun! (2 Corinthians 5:17, NLT)*

If you haven't already made Jesus your LORD and Savior, take a moment now to do it. There is no time like the present because we are not guaranteed tomorrow. It is as easy as praying this simple prayer out loud:

> *Jesus, I believe You are who You say You are—the Son of God. I believe You died on the cross for my sins and I believe God raised You from the dead in victory. I know I have sinned and I repent. I ask Your forgiveness. Please come into my heart, save me, and be the LORD of my life. I am Yours and You are mine. Thank You! Amen.*

If you just prayed that prayer, we are rejoicing with heaven right now. Tell someone. Call a Christian friend, call a local church, or even write our ministry office and let us know so we can be praying for you. It is

Appendix 1 - The Plan of Spiritual Salvation

important that you confess your new salvation to someone else to strengthen your faith. Then, be sure to get into a strong Bible-believing church this Sunday. There's a whole lot more great stuff God has in store for you[203].

Ricky Edwards Ministry
P.O. Box 621
Pawnee, OK 74058

---

[203] Jeremiah 29:11

Faithfulness

Bibliography

"Greek "2962.kurios"." 2004–2016. *BibleHub.com.* 27 July 2016. <http://biblehub.com/greek/2962.htm>.

"Greek "3056.logos"." 2004-2016. *BibleHub.com.* 26 July 2016. <http://biblehub.com/greek/3056.htm>.

Hagin, Kenneth E. *I Believe in Visions.* 2nd Edition. Tulsa: Rhema Bible Church aka Kenneth Hagin Ministries, Inc., 1972, 1984. Softcover. 21 March 2017.

—. *Jesus - The Open Door.* Tulsa: Faith Library Publications, 1996. Print.

—. *Jesus the Open Door.* Tulsa: Faith Shield Publications, 1996. paperback. 17 5 2017.

—. "Kenneth E. Hagin - First Things First." unknown. *Scribd.* PDF Document. 9 December 2016. <https://www.scribd.com/document/182587160/Kenneth-E-Hagin-First-Things-First>.

—. *Understanding the Anointing.* Third Edition. Tulsa: Rhema Bible Church, 1985. Softcover.

—. *Understanding the Anointing.* Broken Arrow: Faith Library Publications, 1985. 21 December 2016. <https://www.scribd.com/doc/47543978/Understanding-the-Anointing-Hagin>.

Holy Bible, Contemporary English Version. Philadelphia: American Bible Society, 1995. Electronic Bible. 28 November 2016. <https://www.biblegateway.com/versions/Contemporary-English-Version-CEV-Bible>.

"Holy Bible, King James Version." 1987. *Bible Gateway.* Ed. Public Domain. Online Bible. 15 September 2015. <https://www.biblegateway.com/versions/King-James-Version-KJV-Bible/>.

"Holy Bible, New Living Translation." copyright © 1996, 2004, 2007. *Bible Gateway.* Ed. Tyndale House Publishers. Tyndale House Foundation, Carol Stream, Illinois 60188. Online Bible. 15 September 2015. <https://www.biblegateway.com/versions/New-Living-Translation-NLT-Bible/>.

"Lackadaisical." 2017. *Dictionary.com Unabridged.* Random House, Inc., 15 March 2017. <http://www.dictionary.com/browse/lackadaisical>.

"Let's Make a Deal." 4 March 2017. *Wikipedia*. Wikimedia Foundation, Inc. 7 March 2017. <https://en.wikipedia.org/wiki/Let%27s_Make_a_Deal>.

"Lily-Livered." n.d. *Dictionary.com Unabridged*. Ed. Inc. Random House. 10 March 2017. <http://www.dictionary.com/browse/lily-livered>.

"maimed." n.d. *Dictionary.com Unabridged*. Random House, Inc. electronic dictionary entry. 7 November 2016. <http://www.dictionary.com/browse/maimed>.

Mays, Jeffery L. "Heaven's Location." n.d. *Remnant Report*. 16 March 2017. <http://remnantreport.com/cgi-bin/imcart/read.cgi?article_id=182>.

Medium. n.d. Merriam-Webster. 9 March 2017. <https://www.merriam-webster.com/dictionary/medium>.

"Mundane." 2017. *Dictionary.com Unabridged*. Random House, Inc. 15 March 2017. <http://www.dictionary.com/browse/mundane>.

"New American Standard Bible." 1960, 1962, 1963, 1968, 1971, 1972, 1973,. *BibleHub*. The Lockman Foundation. 23 May 2017. <http://biblehub.com/nasb/>.

New King James Version. Nashville: Thomas Nelson - HarperCollins Christian Publishing, Inc., 1982. web-based on BibleGateway.com. 11 May 2016. <https://www.biblegateway.com/versions/New-King-James-Version-NKJV-Bible/#booklist>.

Pearson, George. "10 More Days of Prosperity—BVOV Notes." n.d. *Kenneth Copeland Ministries*. 7 March 2017. <http://ftp.kcm.org.za/pdf_downloads/10MoreDaysofProsperity_GeorgePearsons.pdf>.

Pemberton, Garlon. "Abraham's Blessings are Mine." 1985. *SongSelect by CCLI*. NationSong. Lyrics. 27 December 2016. <https://songselect.ccli.com/songs/2489432/abrahams-blessings-are-mine>.

"Rose Garden (Lynn Anderson song)." 18 May 2017. *Wikipedia.com*. 29 May 2017. <https://en.wikipedia.org/wiki/Rose_Garden_(Lynn_Anderson_song)>.

Talley, Dave. "What is Meant by 'these ten times' in Numbers 14:20-23?" 31 March 2014. *The Good Book Blog*. Talbot School of Theology -

Bibliography

Biola University. Blog. 2 December 2016. <http://www.thegoodbookblog.com/2014/mar/31/what-is-meant-by-these-ten-times-in-numbers-1420-2/>.

Thayer's Greek Lexicon. "5485.charis." 2002, 2003, 2006, 2011. *BibleHub.com*. BibleSoft, Inc. Electronic Database. 25 March 2017. <http://biblehub.com/greek/5485.htm>.

"The Bible in Basic English." n.d. *BibleStudyTools.com*. e-Bible. 13 May 2017. <http://www.biblestudytools.com/bbe/>.

The Living Bible. Carol Stream: Tyndale House Publishers, Inc., 1971. e-Bible. 23 April 2016. <https://www.biblegateway.com/versions/The-Living-Bible-TLB/>.

"Weymouth New Testament in Modern Speech." Vers. Third Edition. 1913. *Bible Study Tools*. Ed. Public Domain. Online Bible. 15 September 2015. <http://www.biblestudytools.com/wnt/>.

Winter Bible Seminar 1996-02-22 (IMBF.ORG). Perf. Kennet E. Hagin. Kenneth Hagin Ministries. YouTube Channel: Популярные видео 2013, 1996. Video. 31 March 2017. <https://www.youtube.com/watch?v=AbNqrdTUD70>.

www.ingramcontent.com/pod-product-compliance
Lightning Source LLC
LaVergne TN
LVHW051600070426
835507LV00021B/2675